LOOK UNTO *Me* IN EVERY THOUGHT

JAKOB R. JONES

LOOK UNTO *Me* IN EVERY THOUGHT

CFI
An imprint of Cedar Fort, Inc.
Springville, Utah

Paperback ISBN 13: 978-1-4621-4694-9
eBook ISBN 13: 978-1-4621-4766-3

Published by CFI, an imprint of Cedar Fort, Inc.
2373 W. 700 S., Suite 100, Springville, UT 84663
Distributed by Cedar Fort, Inc., www.cedarfort.com

Library of Congress Control Number: 2024930103

Cover design by Shawnda Craig

Edited and Typeset by Liz Kazandzhy

Printed in the United States of America

10 9 8 7 6 5 4 3 2 1

Printed on acid-free paper

To all those courageously striving to hold on to faith while waiting for answers.

Thank you for your examples.

Contents

Introduction

As members of The Church of Jesus Christ of Latter-day Saints, many of us have had experiences when we've felt the Holy Ghost bear witness to our hearts and minds that the restored gospel is true, that Jesus is the Christ, that Joseph Smith is a prophet of God, and that the Lord guides His Church through living prophets today. Those impressions from the Spirit often come in ways that are hard to forget or ignore. They can leave an indelible mark on us.

Yet even with those spiritual experiences, there can be moments when our testimony of the restored gospel is tested, and we may feel uncertain about the things we once knew to be true.

My friend Amy is a faithful member of the Church and a devoted wife and mother. Amy was raised in the Church and always felt she had a strong testimony of the restored gospel. One day Amy encountered statements about early Church history and Church leaders that surprised her. These new discoveries seemed to contradict the image she'd built up in her mind about the Church and its leaders. She struggled to reconcile this new information with the spiritual confirmations of truth she thought she'd had throughout her life. Amy began to have questions that made her feel uncertain about her testimony. She tried to find answers to her questions, but the sources she studied only increased her concerns, and soon she began to doubt her testimony.

Before long, Amy's doubts began to affect other parts of her life. She found herself questioning the reality of God and the reality of Jesus Christ and His Atonement. Without the hope of Christ's Atonement, she began to lose confidence in herself. Without faith in a loving God, she often worried for her children, fearing that their well-being and safety rested solely on her limited capability to watch over them. She became distrusting of her wonderful husband, a faithful, devoted man. Her marriage became strained. She even began to wonder if she really wanted the life she had chosen as a wife and the mother of her beautiful children. What began with questions soon became a daily struggle with doubt, guilt, confusion, anxiety, and fear.

Amy's story does have a happy ending, and we'll learn more from her experience later. But Amy's story is also not uncommon. You may be able to relate to her. You or someone you love may be struggling with questions, concerns, or doubts about the gospel, about the Lord's restored Church, about Church policies or Church leaders, or even about the reality of the Savior and His Atonement. Such concerns may be affecting your marriage, your family, your personal happiness and sense of peace, or your relationship with our Heavenly Father and His Son, Jesus Christ. Or you may feel that you've just never had a strong testimony of the gospel despite all your efforts to live it.

If you or someone you love is struggling with doubts about their testimony of the gospel, this book is written to you with the hope that something you find here will make a difference—that something here will open the way for you or your loved one to replace doubts and fears with deep faith and conversion.

How do we obtain a lasting testimony of the gospel of Jesus Christ and His restored Church? How do we find answers to our questions? And what do we do when we encounter something that surprises us or causes us to question what we thought we knew to be true? What do we do when those witnesses from the Spirit we've received in the past now feel faint and unsure and all we can feel at the present is fear and disbelief?

Our Savior, Jesus Christ, taught us where to look when these moments arise. "Look unto me in every thought," He said. "Doubt not, fear not" (Doctrine and Covenants 6:36).

This book presents principles that provide a pattern for learning to look to Christ in our moments of doubt and receive answers to our questions. Each chapter contains actions or exercises to help you put these principles into practice. Many of the experiences shared in this book are from Church members, like Amy, who have followed these principles and thereby found their way through the darkness of doubt. They have emerged with brighter testimonies, faith, hope, happiness, joy, and a closeness to our Savior beyond that which they had before their trial of faith. My hope is that these principles will help you or someone you love to do the same.

The Faithful Experience Doubt

"Look unto me in every thought; doubt not, fear not" (Doctrine and Covenants 6:36). The Savior gave those words to Oliver Cowdery and the young Prophet Joseph Smith at a time when Oliver was wrestling with questions of his own regarding the truthfulness of the work of translating the Book of Mormon. The Savior's words are just as applicable to each of us in our own struggles of faith.

Where are we to turn, and who are we to look to, when doubt and fear threaten our testimony of the gospel and our sense of peace? The Savior is clear that we are to look to Him.

One of my favorite paintings tells the New Testament story of Jesus walking on the waters of the Sea of Galilee. In this painting, artist Danny Hahlbohm depicts an ominous sea with high swells and cresting waves. The sky is threatening and dark. Lightning strikes in the distance behind the small ship where Jesus's disciples have been toiling against contrary winds through the night. The Savior is dressed in white, walking calmly upon the sea toward the ship. Out of the dark clouds, a few rays of heavenly light break through to rest upon the confident, serene Christ who seems to emanate a light of His own.

I love the story behind this painting. But my favorite part of the story takes place a few moments after this scene as Jesus nears the ship and invites Peter to join Him on the waters. Peter's experience can teach us much about who may experience doubt, when we can expect to encounter doubt in our lives, and where to look when doubts arise. Here is the account as recorded in the book of Matthew:

> And straightway Jesus constrained his disciples to get into a ship, and to go before him unto the other side, while he sent the multitudes away.
>
> And when he had sent the multitudes away, he went up into a mountain apart to pray: and when the evening was come, he was there alone.
>
> But the ship was now in the midst of the sea, tossed with waves: for the wind was contrary.
>
> And in the fourth watch of the night Jesus went unto them, walking on the sea.
>
> And when the disciples saw him walking on the sea, they were troubled, saying, It is a spirit; and they cried out for fear.
>
> But straightway Jesus spake unto them, saying, Be of good cheer; it is I; be not afraid.
>
> And Peter answered him and said, Lord, if it be thou, bid me come unto thee on the water.
>
> And he said, Come. And when Peter was come down out of the ship, he walked on the water, to go to Jesus.
>
> But when he saw the wind boisterous, he was afraid; and beginning to sink, he cried, saying, Lord, save me.
>
> And immediately Jesus stretched forth his hand, and caught him, and said unto him, O thou of little faith, wherefore didst thou doubt?
>
> And when they were come into the ship, the wind ceased.
>
> Then they that were in the ship came and worshipped him, saying, Of a truth thou art the Son of God. (Matthew 14:22–33)

The Trial of Faith Comes After Receiving a Witness

As I read this story, I am amazed at Peter's great faith. Of all the disciples in the ship, Peter appears to be the only one to have even considered that he might be able to walk on water at the Savior's beckoning. Beyond merely believing, Peter demonstrated enough faith to ask Jesus for such a miracle. It's also worth noting that Peter's request was not private. The rest of the disciples were there in the boat watching. Finally, when the Savior did respond with the invitation to join Him on the water, Peter actually got out of the boat and began walking on that ominous, storm-tossed sea! Peter had enough faith to believe that the Savior could bless him with a miracle, he had sufficient faith to ask for that miracle, he had the faith not to fear what others might think of him, and he had the faith to then act on the Savior's invitation.

Where did this great faith come from? How had Peter developed faith in the Savior sufficient to walk on water, even if only for a few brief moments?

Peter had spent a great deal of time with Jesus listening to His teachings, working alongside Him, and witnessing His miracles. Prior to this experience, consider the many miracles Peter had witnessed Jesus already perform:

- Turning water into wine (see John 2:1–11)
- Healing the dying son of a nobleman (see John 4:46–54)
- Casting out an unclean spirit (see Mark 1:24–27)
- Healing Peter's own mother-in-law (see Matthew 8:14–15)
- Healing many sick people (see Matthew 8:16–17)
- Healing a leper (Matthew 8:1–4)
- Healing a paralytic (see Matthew 9:1–8)
- Healing the servant of a centurion (Matthew 8:5–13)
- Bringing the son of a widow back to life (see Luke 7:11–17)
- Calming a storm on the Sea of Galilee (see Matthew 8:23–27)
- Casting out a legion of evil spirits (see Matthew 8:28–34)
- Raising the daughter of Jairus from the dead (see Matthew 9:18–26)
- Healing the woman with the issue of blood (see Matthew 9:20–22)
- Healing two blind men (see Matthew 9:27–31),
- Restoring speech to a man (see Matthew 9:32–34)

Also, just hours prior to this moment on the water, Peter had witnessed Jesus miraculously feed more than five thousand men, women, and children with five loaves of bread and two fish (see Matthew 14:16–21).

These many spiritual experiences must have contributed to Peter's testimony of the Savior's divinity, power, and teachings. Considering all Peter had seen and experienced, one might ask, as Jesus did after Peter began to sink, "Wherefore didst thou doubt?" (Matthew 14:31). To paraphrase the Savior's question, it's as if to say, "Peter, after everything we've been through together—after everything you've seen and experienced—how can you possibly doubt now?" Yet Peter did experience doubt.

Perhaps Peter's experience with doubt on the Sea of Galilee does not equate perfectly with the trials of testimony-defying doubt you may be experiencing. But just like so many of us—and perhaps like every son and daughter of God experiences at some point in their mortal journey—in a moment of testing and trial, Peter's confidence in himself and in Christ's power, which he'd built out of so many past experiences, wavered. In that moment, fear and doubt briefly overshadowed faith, knowledge, and testimony, and Peter began to sink.

I believe we can find great insight into our own trials of faith by noticing that Peter's trial of faith came *after* he'd already developed a testimony of the Savior. It came *after* all the spiritual witnesses of truth he'd received.

One of the things I learned from my friend Amy is that members of the Church who experience doubts about the gospel often feel a profound sense of guilt. We feel an obligation to be true to what we already know, but we struggle to reconcile those past spiritual experiences with the concerning questions we may presently have. It is not uncommon for members to keep these doubts hidden for fear of what others might think of them or fear of disrupting the faith of their friends and loved ones.

When my friend Amy discussed her faith concerns with her bishop, she was so worried about what he would think of her. She worried about how the Lord felt about her for having doubts. She was genuinely afraid that her doubts made her unworthy. It's true that the Savior has counseled us to "doubt not" (Doctrine and Covenants 6:36). But

Amy was faithfully living the gospel. She was obeying the commandments. She was faithful to her temple covenants. Amy was so relieved when her bishop told her that having questions or concerns about the gospel didn't make her unworthy. It meant she was normal.

Is there something wrong with us when we experience moments when our faith and testimony are tested? Are members of the Church who experience doubt spiritually tainted or broken or incapable of great faith? Does the Savior stop loving us when we struggle at times with our testimony? Peter's experience clearly indicates a resounding no.

President Dieter F. Uchtdorf taught, "There are few members of the Church who, at one time or another, have not wrestled with serious or sensitive questions."[1]

Our past spiritual experiences and witnesses from the Spirit don't preclude us from future trials of faith. The prophet Moroni taught, "Ye receive no witness until after the trial of your faith" (Ether 12:6). But the opposite is also true: we can expect to experience trials of faith *after* we receive a witness of the truth. Faithful Church members who have received a witness can still expect to have moments when their faith and testimony are tested.

As the Savior taught, "My people must be tried in all things, that they may be prepared to receive the glory that I have for them" (Doctrine and Covenants 136:31).

Looking To Christ When Doubts Arise

Just as each of us experiences temptation and hardship in life, every son or daughter of God, no matter how worthy or faithful, may expect to have their faith and testimony tested during their mortal journey. When we or someone we love are wrestling with questions and concerns about the restored gospel, we need to know that such a wrestle is a very normal part of our journey of faith. The question is not whether moments of doubt will potentially arise—the question is what we will do and where we will turn when they do arise.

Where did Peter turn when he began to doubt? When Peter began to sink, he could have looked back to the boat. He could have pleaded

1. Dieter F. Uchtdorf, "Come Join With Us," *Ensign*, Nov. 2013, 23.

with his fellow disciples to rescue him. He could have looked to himself and his own abilities to swim. But he didn't. When Peter was sinking in doubt and fear, his years of past experiences with Christ had trained him where to look for help. He looked to the Savior.

Peter's experience with doubt after receiving so many witnesses of truth was clearly not an indication that he was spiritually incapable of greater faith. After all, this is the man who would eventually lead the Church. This is the man to whom the Savior would give the keys of the kingdom of God on earth after He departed. Later, it is Peter who would be healing the sick and raising the dead such that multitudes would bring their sick to the streets hoping that Peter's shadow would fall on them and heal them (see Acts 5:15). Despite these future great acts, Peter evidently still had something to learn about faith in the Savior.

In fact, as I ponder Peter's experience walking on the sea, I can't help but ask myself a few questions. For example, why did the Savior send His disciples out on the ship in the first place? Surely Christ knew beforehand that they would not make it to the other side alone. The Savior must have known that His disciples would end up struggling against the wind on the storm-tossed sea. Why didn't He then just have them wait for Him on the shore? Christ must have also known Peter well enough to know that this experience would take place. And why did the winds cease *after* they entered the ship? Couldn't Jesus have calmed the storms *before* Peter began to fear and doubt? Couldn't Christ have relieved Peter's fears before they even started, sparing him the entire experience with doubt? The Savior must have known what would transpire and could have altered the circumstances if He'd wanted to. But he didn't. Why?

One must wonder, did the Savior purposefully allow Peter to have this experience as an opportunity to strengthen his faith? Was this experience necessary for the soon-to-be prophet to develop the faith and confidence he would need to fulfill his purposes and calling in life?

It's worth noting that the very next day after this experience on the water, Peter's faith is again tested in the city of Capernaum. The Savior gives a stirring declaration of His divinity as the Son of God in His "bread of life" sermon. John tells us that because these teachings were so difficult for many of Christ's audience to hear, "from that time many of his disciples went back, and walked no more with him" (John 6:66).

The Savior then turned to the Twelve to ask if they too were going to leave Him. It was Peter—impetuous Peter, who only hours before was sinking in doubt—who led the way with faith for his fellow brethren and responded, "Lord, to whom shall we go? thou hast the words of eternal life. And we believe and are sure that thou art that Christ, the Son of the living God" (John 6:68-69).

Wow! How's that for the disciple to whom the Savior had said, only hours before, "O thou of little faith, wherefore didst thou doubt?" (Matthew 14:31). It seems that Peter's test of faith on the Sea of Galilee resulted in an even stronger faith in and testimony of Christ.

If your faith in the restored gospel is being tested, perhaps it's worth asking, "Is this trial of faith something the Savior is intentionally permitting me to experience as an opportunity to increase my faith in Him? Is this part of His plan for me so that I can learn to look to Christ in every thought?"

The Savior said, "I give unto men weakness that they may be humble; and my grace is sufficient for all men that humble themselves before me; for if they humble themselves before me, and have faith in me, then will I make weak things become strong unto them" (Ether 12:27).

Like Peter, if we choose to look to the Savior, our momentary struggle with doubt may lead us to a stronger testimony of the gospel and a stronger relationship with our Savior than we would have otherwise.

Sometime after Amy had learned to look to the Lord to work through her questions, she wrote, "I think I would have drowned if it weren't for the precious conversion I experienced. My faith is stronger than ever. I feel closer to my Savior than ever before. The way I feel about my Heavenly Father has changed so much, and I trust in Him in a way I never did."

Wow! How's that for the faithful daughter of God who, only months earlier, was sinking in doubts of her own?

Where will we turn when doubts threaten our faith? When we wrestle with concerning questions, I believe the Savior stands by, knowing full well our trials and sorrows, waiting patiently for us to reach out to Him and cry, as Peter did, "Lord, save me" (Matthew 14:30).

So we too, in our moments of doubt and fear, must accept the Savior's invitation to "look unto [Him] in every thought" (Doctrine and Covenants 6:36). In doing so, we, like Peter and Amy and so many others, can emerge with greater faith. These experiences can serve to deepen our conversion and testimony. They can result in a closeness to our Heavenly Father and Jesus Christ than we may have experienced otherwise.

Exercises

Ponder the following questions and write down your thoughts.

- What feelings have you experienced when you've encountered something unexpected that caused you to question your faith and testimony in the Lord's Church and restored gospel?
- How do you believe the Savior feels toward those who wrestle with concerns or questions about the restored gospel?
- Consider Peter's experience on the water. In your moments of doubt, where do you currently turn for answers?
- What can you do to look to the Lord for answers to questions?

Principle 1: Seek the Witness of the Holy Ghost

"Eye hath not seen, nor ear heard, neither have entered into the heart of man, the things which God hath prepared for them that love him. But God hath revealed them unto us by his Spirit: for the Spirit searcheth all things, yea, the deep things of God."
(1 Corinthians 2:9–10)

Beth entered her bishop's office. As she sat down, and before either of them spoke, she became emotional as the Spirit filled the room. Over the past many weeks, Beth had been working hard, studying the scriptures, praying, fasting, making personal sacrifices, listening to the words of living prophets and Church leaders, and seeking a personal testimony of the Book of Mormon and the restored gospel.

Beth had grown up in the Church, attended seminary, married in the temple, and served faithfully in many callings, but she never felt she had received a sure witness of the Church and the Book of Mormon. "I've read that book so many times," she had previously told her bishop. "I've prayed to ask if it's true, just like you're supposed to do, and I've never gotten an answer. I feel like if it were true, I should have gotten an answer." Beth also struggled to feel God's love for her, and she wasn't truly happy. At some point Beth had kind of given up trying to develop a testimony.

But the Lord had not given up on Beth. Her bishop received several promptings that the Lord wanted Beth to experience greater joy, peace, and spiritual potential in her life. The Lord wanted Beth to feel His love for her. At her bishop's invitation, Beth decided to give the Lord another chance. She accepted assignments to help her learn more about herself and her relationship with her Savior and to seek a witness of the restored gospel. She began a sincere, prayerful study of the Book of Mormon.

Now, in her bishop's office, after several weeks of sincere effort, Beth was receiving part of the answer she'd been seeking. "I feel like I'm getting my answer," she said through tears. "I feel like the Lord is telling me, 'Beth, you already know the answer. You know the Book of Mormon is true, so stop asking me.'"

Perhaps that feels like a strange answer for you or me. But for Beth, this was a sweet and an important moment. She experienced a closeness to her Heavenly Father and her Savior that she needed. This experience, along with others, confirmed for Beth that the Lord loved her and that she could receive answers to her questions. What made that experience so important was not the answer itself; it was the source of the answer. In that moment, years of doubt and fear were replaced with feelings of love, peace, and confidence. Beth was receiving revelation. She was receiving a divine witness of truth from heaven through the Holy Ghost.

The Source of All Truth

When Jesus walked the earth during His mortal ministry, His disciples could personally ask Him their most important and challenging questions. But the Savior knew the time would come when He would no longer be physically present to respond to their questions. Here is the counsel He gave them when He knew that time was drawing near: "These things have I spoken unto you, being yet present with you. But the Comforter, which is the Holy Ghost, whom the Father will send in my name, he shall teach you all things, and bring all things to your remembrance, whatsoever I have said unto you" (John 14:25–26).

The Holy Ghost is that member of the Godhead whose mission it is to reveal divine knowledge and truth to us. He is sent from the

Father in the name of Christ. It is through the Holy Ghost that we can know all things if we learn to humbly seek and recognize His voice.

Only divine revelation from heaven can bring the closeness with our Heavenly Father that our spirits need. Only that witness can quiet the confusing voices of the world, satisfy the questions that matter most, and bring peace to replace doubt. No earthly answer will suffice.

So our first principle in overcoming doubt and receiving answers to important questions of faith is to understand that what we are really searching for is a divine witness of truth from heaven. And that witness can only come through the Holy Ghost.

We start with this principle because it is the undertone for all our subsequent principles and efforts. The purpose of all our searching, pondering, and studying is to create within us an environment where the Holy Ghost can bear witness of the truth to our hearts. This first principle guides us in what we study, how we study, what questions we ask, how we ask, and who we ask. It will guide our actions and decisions as we patiently seek answers from a loving Heavenly Father.

Earthly Answers Are Insufficient

President Henry B. Eyring of the First Presidency taught, "The truth that matters most is verified only by revelation from God. Our human reason and the use of our physical senses will not be enough. We live in a time when even the wisest will be hard-pressed to distinguish truth from clever deception."[2]

Most members of the Church understand the Spirit's role as a revelator of truth. Many of us have been taught about the Holy Ghost since our days in Primary. We sing about it in our sacrament meetings. Those who served a full-time mission spent time teaching others how to seek a testimony through the Holy Ghost.

Yet it is not uncommon for even the most faithful, knowledgeable Latter-day Saints to get stuck in a pattern of looking to sources other than God to resolve their spiritual doubts and questions.

---

2. Henry B. Eyring, "The Holy Ghost as Your Companion," *Ensign*, Nov. 2015, 105.

As I have watched friends in the Church struggle with questions that threaten their testimony of the restored gospel, I have observed that those who successfully emerge with a burning testimony of faith are those who, like Beth, are willing to sincerely give Heavenly Father a chance to answer their questions and guide their lives through revelation rather than relying solely on the commentary and wisdom of others.

Remember my friend Amy? Amy's struggle with her testimony of the restored gospel originated with things she encountered on the internet. Amy then entered a long struggle, desperately searching for more information to resolve her doubts. But she mostly went to the internet, looking for answers among the opinions of others and trying to find information that would prove or disprove her fears. There she found ample commentary from some faithful Church members, struggling Church members, disaffected Church members, angry Church members, and people who have never been members of the Church but who nevertheless held strong opinions.

The problem for Amy was that, after immersing herself in all this information and biased commentary, she couldn't distinguish what was true from what was false. And even when she did encounter information that appeared true, even if it seemed negative, she wasn't sure how to process it or how that information fit with the witnesses of the gospel she'd previously received throughout her life. She began to question the spiritual experiences she'd had in the past. Over time it became more difficult to recognize the voice of the Spirit. And instead of getting closer to finding answers to her questions, she became more confused, more doubtful, and more filled with anxiety, and she felt less and less at peace.

Where Amy got stuck, and where many of us can get lost, is that she didn't know how to balance all that earthly information and commentary by also going to the Lord for answers and direction. She fell into the trap of mistakenly believing that the answers must be somewhere there among all that human reasoning. Amy's *heart* was in the right place—she just needed help to learn how to look to the Savior in all her *thoughts* to receive answers to her questions.

Amy's experience is all too common. It is so easy for us to become stuck in this perpetual cycle of "ever learning, [but] never able to come to the knowledge of the truth" (2 Timothy 3:7). This cycle can be spiritually and emotionally exhausting. For many Church members, the very foundations of our beliefs, values, and family relationships feel threatened in such a faith crisis. And too many Church members eventually give up, assuming they just can't obtain the answers they need among the confusion.

It's so important for those going through such a wrestle to know they are not alone. In such moments, we can identify well with the experience young Joseph Smith described in his search for truth among the opinions of men:

> So great were the confusion and strife among the different denominations, that it was impossible for a person young as I was, and so unacquainted with men and things, to come to any certain conclusion who was right and who was wrong. . . .
>
> In the midst of this war of words and tumult of opinions, I often said to myself: What is to be done? Who of all these parties are right; or, are they all wrong together? If any one of them be right, which is it, and how shall I know it? (Joseph Smith—History 1:8, 10)

We all likely know someone—a family member, friend, or a beloved ward member—who has become so frustrated in searching for answers to their questions of faith among earthly evidence that they just feel like giving up or already have.

If you or someone you love are close to giving up on trying to resolve your questions and doubts about the Lord's restored Church, I plead with you to hold on! Don't give up yet! Having witnessed the experience in myself and countless others, I promise that you can find the answers you need. The Lord loves us. He wants to give the peace we are desperately seeking. He wants you to feel of His love for you. He knows what you are going through and promises not to leave you comfortless if you will turn to Him (see John 14:18). Sometimes, like Beth and Amy, we just need a little help to know how to clear away the confusion, to prepare our hearts to hear His voice, and to look unto Him in all our thoughts.

You'll recall that young Joseph Smith's breakthrough finally came when he understood that he could ask God directly for answers instead of relying on the perspectives of men (see Joseph Smith—History 1:11–13). That discovery eventually led to the peace and personal relationship with God that Joseph was so desperately seeking.

Joseph later taught, "Could you gaze into heaven five minutes, you would know more than you would by reading all that ever was written on the subject."[3]

We must all eventually make that same discovery. If we are to find peace and come to know God, each of us must eventually acknowledge that our search for truth requires us to put aside the opinions of men, stop relying solely on our own intellect and reason, and turn instead toward God, seeking a witness of the truth through His Spirit.

Revelation Requires Work

After Beth's experience receiving her desired witness of the Book of Mormon, she wrote, "I find getting revelation to be an overwhelming and daunting task. I will work hard to obtain the ability to receive it. I find that I am needing to learn who God is and how He works."

While the answers we seek must come from heaven, receiving revelation does require work on our part. We cannot rely alone on our reason and intellect for answers to spiritual questions, but we must bring the best of our reason, intellect, and effort in our search for truth.

Elder David A. Bednar taught:

> A learner exercising agency by acting in accordance with correct principles opens his or her heart to the Holy Ghost and invites His teaching, testifying power, and confirming witness. Learning by faith requires spiritual, mental, and physical exertion and not just passive reception. It is in the sincerity and consistency of our faith-inspired action that we indicate to our Heavenly Father and His Son, Jesus Christ, our willingness to learn and receive instruction from the Holy Ghost.[4]

---

3. *Teachings of the Prophet Joseph Smith*, sel. Joseph Fielding Smith (1976), 324.

4. David A, Bednar, "Seek Learning by Faith", *Ensign*, Sept. 2007, 64.

Elder Bednar's instruction makes it clear that preparing ourselves to be taught by the Holy Ghost requires action and effort. Look at the action words in his statements:

- "act" in accordance with correct principles
- "open" our hearts to the Holy Ghost
- "invite" the Spirit's power and witness
- "exertion" (spiritual, mental, and physical)
- "sincere" and "consistent" faith-inspired "action"
- "indicate" our willingness to the Father and His Son
- "receive" instruction

Those statements indicate intentional effort on our part to receive revelation. Our Heavenly Father loves us. He stands ready to help us and provide answers. But He will not force truth upon us, nor will He bestow it upon those who do not sincerely intend to act upon it. We demonstrate our willingness and preparation to receive truth through doing the right work.

The work we do in our search for truth, however, is not to scour the internet looking for earthly answers to our questions. We cannot put effort into planting oranges if we hope to harvest apples. Instead, our work is to prepare our hearts and minds to receive truth by revelation through the Holy Ghost. That work creates the conditions and environment within us so that we are worthy, willing, receptive, and prepared to hear and discern the Lord's voice and act on it. The remaining principles we will study in this book can teach us how to do that work.

President Russel M. Nelson taught, "My beloved brothers and sisters, I plead with you to increase your spiritual capacity to receive revelation. . . . Choose to do the spiritual work required to enjoy the gift of the Holy Ghost and hear the voice of the Spirit more frequently and more clearly."[5]

---

5. Russell M. Nelson, "Revelation for the Church, Revelation for Our Lives," *Ensign*, May 2018, 96.

Giving the Lord a Chance

As a bishop, when faithful friends or ward members would share with me their doubts and questions about the restored gospel, I would first let them know that they were not alone, that the Lord loved them for wanting to do the right thing, and that it was okay that they were struggling. I would try to reassure them that the Lord could bring them the peace they were seeking.

I would then often feel impressed to ask something like, "What would you like to do? Would you like to receive a testimony? Would you be willing to give the Lord a chance to give you that witness? Are you willing to spend some time seeking answers from the Holy Ghost? It would involve sincerely studying the scriptures and the words of living prophets, keeping the commandments, asking the Lord sincere questions in prayer, and repenting of sins. You'd have to show the Lord you're willing to follow Him. You don't need to be perfect, but would you be willing to do some things to put forth that effort?"

Some individuals would honestly respond with "I'm not interested" or "I don't know if I can right now." And that's okay. I believe the Lord stands ready to receive us when we're ready to reach out to Him. But for those who were ready to sincerely try, I was privileged to witness that the Lord rewards even our smallest efforts with miracles in our lives far beyond a strengthened testimony. Those who were ready to "look unto [Christ] in every thought" (Doctrine and Covenants 6:36), and who showed their faith in Him through their sincere effort, developed a closer relationship with the Savior than they'd ever experienced before.

In the following chapters we'll discuss how we can act in faith so that the Lord can give us that witness. Are we willing to put forth that effort? If we're at least willing to try, that's enough to start.

Exercises

Ponder the following questions and write down your thoughts.

- What sources have you been going to for answers to spiritual questions? Are these sources bringing peace? Do they draw you closer to your Heavenly Father?

- What do you learn from the following verses regarding how we receive a divine witness of truth? 1 Corinthians 2:9–14; John 16:13; Alma 5:45–47; Moroni 10:4–5; Jacob 7:12.
- Elder Bednar talked about the work we must put in to prepare ourselves and demonstrate our readiness and willingness to receive a witness of truth through the Holy Ghost. What personal promptings has the Holy Ghost given you regarding things you can do or change to prepare yourself to receive answers from heaven? Have you acted on those promptings?

Principle 2: Remember How Merciful the Lord Hath Been

"O give thanks unto the Lord; for he is good; for his mercy endureth for ever." (1 Chronicles 16:34)

Near the end of the Book of Mormon are a few verses that most Church members are very familiar with. They are found in Moroni 10:3–5, and we often refer to them as "Moroni's promise." As a missionary serving in Costa Rica, I must have shared those words hundreds of times with the people I taught. The basic message of these verses, as we usually explain it, is that if someone will read the Book of Mormon and ask God if it is true, they can receive a divine witness of its truth by the power of the Holy Ghost.

However, we often overlook something very important in the process of receiving that witness. Let's look at only the first verse of Moroni's promise. It says, "Behold, I would exhort you that when ye shall read these things, if it be wisdom in God that ye should read them, that ye would . . . remember how merciful the Lord hath been unto the children of men, from the creation of Adam even down until the time that ye shall receive these things, and ponder it in your hearts" (Moroni 10:3).

What is the first thing Moroni exhorts us to do once we've received the words found in the Book of Mormon? It is to remember and ponder God's mercy. Why would Moroni suggest remembering

God's mercy toward His children as an important step in receiving a witness of truth through the Holy Ghost? What does remembering God's mercy have anything to do with our testimony of the Book of Mormon and the restored gospel?

God's Mercy toward Us

Author Brad Wilcox shared a story in his book *The Continuous Atonement* that I believe highlights how our testimony can be affected when we forget God's mercy toward us. While Brother Wilcox was serving as a bishop of a student ward at Brigham Young University, a young man in his ward came to visit him. The young man opened up and confessed sins that he'd been carrying since his youth but had never been able to tell another bishop or other priesthood leader. After confessing and counseling and studying the Atonement with Bishop Wilcox that evening, the young man left feeling like a tremendous burden had been lifted from him. He felt changed and freed from his sins.

But for the next two Sundays, this young man did not show up for church. Finally, out of concern, Bishop Wilcox decided to visit him at his apartment. Here is the exchange that followed as Brother Wilcox recounts:

> The young man answered the door but didn't invite me in. His countenance was dark. His eyes were hollow. His comments were negative and sarcastic, revealing his depression. I asked if I could come in and talk with him.
>
> He said, "Like that will make any difference." His words were cold and hard. "Just face it, Bishop, the Church isn't true. No one can even prove there is a God. It's all just a joke, so don't waste your time."[6]

Bishop Wilcox continues:

> I had one of those bishop moments: I knew what was wrong. Rather than raising my voice or quoting scripture, I simply said, "You messed up again, didn't you?"

---

6. Brad Wilcox, *The Continuous Atonement* (Salt Lake City, UT: Deseret Book, 2009), Deseret Bookshelf.

> His darkened expression melted, and this young returned missionary began to cry. Between sobs he motioned me into his empty apartment, where we sat together on the couch. He said, "Bishop, I'm sorry. I just feel so bad. I finally repented. I was finally clean. I finally put it all behind me. I finally used the Atonement, and it felt so good. Then I blew it all over again. Now my former sins have returned, and I feel like the worst person in the world."
>
> I asked, "So the Church is true and there is a God after all?"
>
> "Of course," he responded sheepishly.
>
> "So you just need another chance?"[7]

What was it that caused this young man's sudden loss of faith and testimony? Had the Church changed? Had God ceased to exist? Were all his past spiritual experiences suddenly no longer valid? No. All it took for this young man to doubt his past spiritual experiences and be consumed with despair was to forget that God's mercy and Christ's Atonement were still available to him, even after he messed up.

This young man had temporarily lost sight of God's loving mercy for him. He had temporarily lost hope in Christ's ability to change him no matter how many times he faltered. And without that hope in God's mercy for him personally, it became impossible for him to see God's mercy for anyone or anything else. Without that mercy, he couldn't believe in a loving God, in a restored Church guided by a living Christ, and in living prophets and apostles.

Bishop Wilcox spent the evening teaching and reminding this young man that Christ's grace was sufficient to allow him as many chances as he needed, so long as he kept trying.

Forgetting God's Mercy Can Lead to Doubt

We all have such a long way to go on our road to perfection. We fall short in so many ways along that road. We sometimes forget that the purpose of this life is to learn and grow through experience, not to display a flawless performance.

As a bishop, I would often discover that a member's doubts about the Church coincided with a time when they were going through a personal struggle with sin, perfectionism, guilt, or just feeling like

---

7. Wilcox, *The Continuous Atonement*, chap. 1.

they didn't fit into the Lord's Church. Among the most destructive tactics that Satan uses to destroy faith, perhaps none is more effective than to convince us that because of our sins and mistakes, we are no longer worthy of the Lord's mercy. What could destroy faith and hope more quickly than to be convinced that we're not worth saving, that we've fallen beyond the reach of Christ's Atonement and God's love for us, that we're too far gone?

We should understand that Satan will use those feelings of hopelessness to create doubt. If Satan can convince us to doubt God's mercy for us, we may soon begin to see everything and everyone else around us with that same lack of mercy. Soon we start looking for and finding fault everywhere around us—in ourselves, loved ones, Church leaders, prophets, apostles, Church policies, and on and on.

Truly this is the gall of bitterness: feeling no hope for personal redemption or happiness and thus being bent on denying such for everyone else. We should note that this is exactly the bitterness that Satan himself feels. Lehi teaches us that "because [Satan] had fallen from heaven, and had become miserable forever, he sought also the misery of all mankind" (2 Nephi 2:18), and that "he seeketh that all men might be miserable like unto himself" (2 Nephi 2:27). Having consciously chosen to reject all that God offers, and having given up all hope of real happiness, Satan seeks to find misery in as much company as possible by convincing us that we are in the same hopeless situation he has chosen.

This is where our testimony becomes vulnerable. In our moment of misery, Satan tries to convince us that doubt is actually the solution to our problem. His reasoning goes something like this: "If the Church isn't true, and if God doesn't exist, then the way out of this misery and guilt you're feeling is to simply walk away from it all." Instead of looking to Christ for healing when we most desperately need it, Satan would have us turn away from everything the Savior has put in place to help us: His Church, prophets, apostles, stake presidents and bishops, the scriptures, the priesthood, saving ordinances, the commandments, temples, prayer, and so on.

By sowing the seed of doubting God's mercy for us, Satan can succeed in severing us from the very things the Savior has put in place to save us. He can succeed in blocking us from receiving revelation from the Holy Ghost.

Looking To Christ When We Fall Short

When we are confronted with our own shortcomings, instead of turning to doubt, we can honor Moroni's plea to remember God's mercy toward us and also the Savior's plea to "look unto [Him] in every thought" (Doctrine and Covenants 6:36).

I have had more than one faithful, struggling friend express to me their worries that perhaps they are beyond the reach of Christ's Atonement. They've said it in different ways: "I'm not good enough." "I'm not smart enough." "I make too many mistakes." "I don't measure up." "I don't think Christ can fix me after everything I've done." "The blessings of forgiveness and eternal life talked about in the scriptures might apply to other Church members but not to me."

Elder Jeffrey R. Holland taught, "However late you think you are, however many chances you think you have missed, however many mistakes you feel you have made or talents you think you don't have, or however far from home and family and God you feel you have traveled, I testify that you have not traveled beyond the reach of divine love. It is not possible for you to sink lower than the infinite light of Christ's Atonement shines."[8]

If we, dear brothers and sisters, find we have fallen into this trap of believing that Christ either no longer wants us or can no longer rescue us—if we have temporarily lost sight of God's mercy for us—I invite each of us to personally take to heart these words from Christ Himself: "I say unto you, if ye will come unto me ye shall have eternal life. Behold, mine arm of mercy is extended towards you, and whosoever will come, him will I receive; and blessed are those who come unto me" (3 Nephi 9:14).

While I was serving as a bishop, a wonderful brother came to visit with me in the office one evening. Many years prior, as a young returned missionary, John had become inactive in the Church. It was partly due to a list of doubts about the Church but largely because temptations had drawn John toward actions that led him to violate

---

8. Jeffrey R. Holland, "The Laborers in the Vineyard," *Ensign*, May 2012, 33.

his baptismal and temple covenants. While he was growing up in a strong Latter-day Saint home, the rules and commandments of the gospel felt restrictive and oppressive to him, and he longed for what he thought would be freedom from those restrictions. Acting on those desires led him to years of inactivity, immorality, and substance abuse.

Now—after long years of maturing through life, marriage, and having children—John sat before his bishop with increased perspective and an appreciation for what the Church had been trying to provide him and protect him from when he was younger. He opened his heart and listed out the doubts he'd had about the Church, which, even as he spoke them, seemed to fade into irrelevance with his new perspective. And as he spoke, the real and most important question on his mind came to the surface: "After all I've done, is it even possible for me to come back?"

Can you imagine how the Savior feels about someone in this moment? I was overwhelmed with Christ's love for this young son of God. "Oh, John," I told him. "Our Savior is so good and so kind and so loving. He is so patient with us. He's not punitive. All He wants is for us to have the opportunity to be happy, to be forgiven, to be changed. That's why He did what He did for us. That's why He went into the Garden of Gethsemane for us. He knew what we were going to do before He went in there, and He still went in willingly. And the instant that any one of us sincerely turns to Him and asks for His help, He immediately opens His arms to receive us. That is His nature."

I continued, "John, if you want to be back, you're back. Yes, you and I have some things to work on, but that's fine—that's what the Atonement is for. There is nothing here that you have done that the Savior can't fix. And these doubts you've expressed are common, and we can work on those. They shouldn't stop you from coming back. John, if you want to be back, you're back. So . . . welcome back, John."

Tears came as the Holy Ghost helped John remember the reality of God's mercy for him. John did return to church, and he brought his young family with him. John still doesn't have answers to all his questions, but he had his most important question answered. Remembering and personally experiencing God's mercy was an essential step in allowing John to move forward in faith.

Receiving a Personal Witness of God's Mercy

Those who have personally experienced God's mercy through the healing power of Christ's Atonement develop unshakable testimonies of faith and are able to bear powerful witness to the divinity of the Savior and His ability to save.

The prophet Nephi wrote, "I glory in truth; I glory in my Jesus, for he hath redeemed my soul" (2 Nephi 33:6). And after Alma tasted of Christ's mercy, he testified, "I have repented of my sins, and have been redeemed of the Lord; behold I am born of the Spirit" (Mosiah 27:24). He later testified to his son Helaman, "I know that [God] will raise me up at the last day, to dwell with him in glory; yea, and I will praise him forever" (Alma 36:28).

When we have personally been redeemed through the mercy of Christ's Atonement, we are changed. Our demeanors change. Our countenances change. Our desires and motivations change. We become more kind, more patient, more loving. We become free from the heavy burdens of sin, doubt, and fear. We begin to lose our fear of the world, knowing that Christ has overcome the world (see John 16:33). This change in us is essential to our testimony. Doubt and fear have a more difficult time grabbing hold of us when we personally experience the gradual change of being redeemed through Christ's Atonement.

Moroni's final words in the Book of Mormon are an invitation to experience this change and obtain this undeniable witness. He said, "Yea, come unto Christ, and be perfected in him, and deny yourselves of all ungodliness; and if ye shall deny yourselves of all ungodliness, and love God with all your might, mind and strength, then is his grace sufficient for you, that by his grace ye may be perfect in Christ; and if by the grace of God ye are perfect in Christ, ye can in nowise deny the power of God" (Moroni 10:32).

We are not perfect, but Christ is. And because of His grace and mercy, we can be perfect in Christ right now—today. We can have the confidence that Nephi and Alma had, knowing that Christ can and will save us. We can know that we are claimed by His Atonement and that we are securely on the path of being gradually perfected by Him. His grace is sufficient for us now. And when we've personally experienced God's grace and mercy, we cannot deny the power of God in our life.

Moroni's plea to remember God's mercy toward His children is an essential principle in preparing our hearts to receive an enduring witness of Jesus Christ and His restored gospel. When our imperfections, shortcomings, and sins tempt us to lose hope and give into doubt, we can instead choose to look to the Savior in those thoughts. We can choose to let Him heal us. We can choose to remember how merciful the Lord has been.

Exercises

Ponder the following questions and write down your thoughts.

- Read and ponder the following verses: 2 Nephi 26:24–28; 3 Nephi 9:14,17, 20–22; Alma 5:33; John 3:15–16; John 12:46–47. As you read, try to apply the verses as if the Lord or His servants are speaking directly to you, and consider the following questions:
    - Who does the Savior invite to come unto Him?
    - Who is he willing to receive?
    - What is the only thing Christ asks for in return?
    - How does this apply to you personally?
- Have you had moments when a recognition of your shortcomings or sins have caused you to give up hope, or to doubt the Lord's love for you or your testimony of the gospel? Where do you think these feelings of doubt originate?
- Make a list of the moments when you've experienced God's mercy in your life. How do these experiences affect your testimony of Heavenly Father, Jesus Christ, the Holy Ghost, and the Lord's Church?
- Many Church members may struggle with perfectionism. Perfectionism includes the mistaken belief that our worth, value, and God's love for us is dependent on our performance in life. Perfectionism limits our ability to act for fear of acting imperfectly. It limits our ability to find peace and prevents us from letting Christ in to heal and change us. Satan can also use per-

fectionism to keep us stuck in self-doubt and guilt when we fall short of our own unrealistic expectations. Perfectionism can affect our testimony of Heavenly Father, Jesus Christ, and the restored gospel. The topic of perfectionism merits a book of its own, and often those who struggle with it may require professional counseling as part of their healing process. If you are struggling with perfectionism, consider reading or listening to the following resources as a start, and write down what you learn.

- Brad Wilcox, "His Grace Is Sufficient" (Brigham Young University devotional, July 12, 2011), speeches.byu.edu.
- Tyler J. Jarvis, "That's How the Light Gets In" (Brigham Young University devotional, July 9, 2013), speeches.byu.edu.

If There Are Faults

I believe Moroni had another important reason for asking us to ponder God's mercy in order to receive a witness of truth. Recall that Moroni's plea was to "remember how merciful the Lord hath been unto the children of men, from the creation of Adam even down until the time that ye shall receive these things, and ponder it in your hearts" (Moroni 10:3).

As I ponder Moroni's writings in the Book of Mormon, I think his request was partially motivated by a particular worry. Consider Moroni's words in the following passages, and see if you recognize his concern.

Here it is as he expressed it to the Savior, as recorded in the book of Ether: "Lord, the Gentiles will mock at these things, because of our weakness. . . . When we write we behold our weakness, and stumble because of the placing of our words; and I fear lest the Gentiles shall mock at our words" (Ether 12:23, 25).

In Moroni's first words to us in Mormon 8, he wrote, "And whoso receiveth this record, and shall not condemn it because of the imperfections which are in it, the same shall know of greater things than these" (Mormon 8:12).

Finally, he engraved these words on the title page of the Book of Mormon: "And now, if there are faults they are the mistakes of men; wherefore, condemn not the things of God."

Moroni's words reveal a persistent worry that his personal weaknesses and imperfections, and the weaknesses of those who had written before him, would make it difficult for you and me to receive the Book of Mormon and the restored gospel. I believe he worried that we would not be able to see past the human weakness of the Lord's servants enough to see Christ working through them.

Moroni's fears are not unique. A review of the stories of ancient prophets reveals that it is common among the Lord's prophets to worry about their own weaknesses interfering with the work of God.

For example, when the Lord called upon Moses to lead the children of Israel, he responded, "But, behold, they will not believe me, nor hearken unto my voice. . . . O my Lord, I am not eloquent, . . . but I am slow of speech, and of a slow tongue" (Genesis 4:1, 10). Enoch, upon receiving his call, questioned, "Why is it that I have found favor in thy sight, and am but a lad, and all the people hate me; for I am slow of speech; wherefore am I thy servant?" (Moses 6:31). Isaiah, after seeing the Lord and being called to serve, lamented, "Woe is me! for I am undone; because I am a man of unclean lips" (Isaiah 6:5). And when the Lord called Jeremiah, he exclaimed, "Ah, Lord God! behold, I cannot speak: for I am a child" (Jeremiah 1:6).

Such worries are not limited to prophets. Perhaps every Church member experiences the fear that their own imperfections may prevent others from seeing Christ in the work.

Shortly after I was called to serve as a bishop, I shared my own concerns with the stake president. The prior bishop had been so charismatic and well loved, and he had done such a wonderful job. "I just don't want anything about me to be a stumbling block for the members of the ward," I said. At that time, I needed to develop my own faith that the Savior could work through me despite my many imperfections.

Moroni's concerns have proven to be quite valid. The fact that God calls upon imperfect men and women to lead His Church has been a great obstacle for many Church members.

My friend Amy's biggest challenge to her testimony of the restored gospel began when she encountered information on the internet about Joseph Smith and other early Church leaders that did not align with her expectations of the Lord's servants. She struggled to reconcile how these men and women could have been called of God when she couldn't understand or agree with their purported actions.

Another very good friend shared that his faith was tested when a fellow ward member, whose mistakes and weaknesses he was familiar with, was called to serve as his bishop. "I'm going to need some time," he said, meaning he needed time for the Spirit to confirm to him that this calling came from God—and perhaps time to forgive his new bishop for some of the past offenses between them.

We all likely know someone whose trial of faith is rooted in concern over the imperfect actions or characters of past or present Church leaders or members. Because it's almost certain that we will encounter this particular challenge to our testimony at some point, it's important to remember Moroni's concerns and this aspect of the Lord's mercy.

How can we have faith sufficient to stay close to the Lord's Church and receive the Lord's will through His servants when we know that human imperfection is inherent in the work? The answer, again, lies in learning to look unto Christ.

I believe Moroni is making a sincere plea to us to remember that from the beginning of time, God's mercy has always included His ability to accomplish His work through imperfect but willing servants. Developing an enduring testimony of the restored gospel will require each of us to obtain our own witness from the Holy Ghost that Christ is able to lead and guide His Church even through human frailties. We can begin to develop that testimony as we ponder and understand God's mercy and strive to develop some measure of that mercy within ourselves.

The Lord Calls Upon the Weak and Simple

Elder M. Russell Ballard stated, "Too many people think Church leaders and members should be perfect or nearly perfect. They forget that the Lord's grace is sufficient to accomplish His work through mortals. Our leaders have the best intentions, but sometimes we make mistakes. . . . Looking for human weakness in others is rather easy. However, we make a serious mistake by noticing only the human nature of one another and then failing to see God's hand working through those He has called."[9]

In the Lord's preface to the Doctrine and Covenants—effectively His opening message to the world regarding the Restoration of the gospel in the latter days—the Savior acknowledged the weaknesses of His servants. In describing why He called upon and gave revelations to Joseph Smith and others to restore the Church, the Lord revealed some of the reasons why He calls upon the weak and simple to accomplish His work. He said, "The weak things of the world shall come forth and break down the mighty and strong ones, that man should not counsel his fellow man, neither trust in the arm of flesh—But that every man might speak in the name of God the Lord, even the Savior of the world; That faith also might increase in the earth" (Doctrine and Covenants 1:19–21).

These statements from the Savior indicate that the Lord's calling of imperfect men and women to accomplish His work is intentional, and it's partly meant to shift our focus away from the strength and capabilities of men and instead focus our faith and trust in God. Ironically, the calling of imperfect servants is meant to *increase* our faith in the Lord's work rather than diminish it.

Speaking of modern prophets and apostles, Elder David A. Bednar taught, "Interestingly, the mortal limitations of these men actually affirm the divine source of the revelations that come to and through them."[10]

And Moroni, in a final petition to his readers on this subject, pleads with us, "Condemn me not because of mine imperfection, neither my father, because of his imperfection, neither them who have written before him; but rather give thanks unto God that he hath made manifest unto you our imperfections, that ye may learn to be more wise than we have been" (Mormon 9:31).

In order for God to accomplish His purposes in the lives of His children, it is essential that our faith be in Christ and not in men. As Peter taught, "There is none other name under heaven given among

---

9. M. Russell Ballard, "God Is at the Helm," *Ensign*, Nov. 2015, 25.

10. David A. Bednar, "Chosen to Bear Testimony of My Name," *Ensign*, Nov. 2015, 129.

men, whereby we must be saved" (Acts 4:12). What might happen if the Lord were to send perfected men and women to lead His Church? Might we then be tempted to put our faith and trust in *them* instead of looking to Christ, something we're perhaps already guilty of at times? Observing the Lord's ability to work through mortal men and women should remind us that the Savior stands at the head of His Church and directs the work.

Returning to section 1 of the Doctrine and Covenants, the Lord cited other reasons for calling upon the weak and the simple in this work:

> That mine everlasting covenant might be established;
>
> That the fulness of my gospel might be proclaimed by the weak and the simple unto the ends of the world, and before kings and rulers.
>
> Behold, I am God and have spoken it; these commandments are of me, and were given unto my servants in their weakness, after the manner of their language, that they might come to understanding.
>
> And inasmuch as they erred it might be made known;
>
> And inasmuch as they sought wisdom they might be instructed;
>
> And inasmuch as they sinned they might be chastened, that they might repent;
>
> And inasmuch as they were humble they might be made strong, and blessed from on high, and receive knowledge from time to time. (Doctrine and Covenants 1:22–28)

These statements indicate that our personal growth and development are central to the way the Lord chooses to organize His kingdom here on earth. The Lord is intentional about including all of us in His work for our learning and benefit. He permits us to make mistakes and repent, to be chastened and refined, and to learn and grow as we serve Him and each other in this great work. The Lord does not pretend that our sins and weaknesses do not exist, but He does provision for them.

This truth has some obvious and challenging implications for us as Church members. It means that from time to time, we're going to bump into each other with our imperfections. It means we will sometimes offend each other. It means we won't get everything right as we do this work. It means the door is open for those in leadership positions to act on their own ideas rather than dictation from the Holy Ghost. It means the Lord will sometimes allow us to make incorrect decisions and go down incorrect paths long enough to learn from them. It means that Church programs may not always run smoothly. It means the work will sometimes appear messy and imperfect.

Why does the Lord allow all this disorder and chaos? It helps to remember that Christ's objective is not a flawless, smoothly running church organization where no one has cause to question and no mistakes are made. His objective is *us*. It is to "bring about the immortality and eternal life of man [and woman]" (Moses 1:39). We all get to be a part of the work; it's necessary for our progression and learning. Our weaknesses allow Christ to demonstrate His redemptive power. Through our weaknesses, Christ is glorified and we are made strong (see Ether 12:27).

Christ is intensely merciful and patient with us as we go through this process. We must acknowledge that if human imperfection is part of the plan, then an enduring testimony of the Lord's restored Church will require us, at least in some measure, to see the work through the same lens of mercy through which God sees it.

Elder Jeffrey R. Holland gave the following counsel regarding developing such mercy:

> Be kind regarding human frailty—your own as well as that of those who serve with you in a Church led by volunteer, mortal men and women. Except in the case of His only perfect Begotten Son, imperfect people are all God has ever had to work with. That must be terribly frustrating to Him, but He deals with it. So should we. And when you see imperfection, remember that the limitation is not in the divinity of the work. As one gifted writer has suggested, when the infinite fulness is poured forth, it is not the oil's fault if there is some loss because finite vessels can't quite contain it all. Those finite vessels include you and me, so be patient and kind and forgiving.[11]

In those moments when our faith is tested because of what we perceive to be human imperfection in the Church, we can choose to replace our fears with an increase of trust in God's mercy. We can

11. Jeffrey R. Holland, "Lord, I Believe," *Ensign*, May 2013, 94.

choose to trust that Christ sees the end from the beginning, and we can strive to view His imperfect servants, including ourselves, with that same patience and mercy that He chooses to view us with.

By the Voice of My Servants

While the Lord acknowledges imperfection in His servants, He also makes it clear that we are to receive His word through them. During the final evening with His disciples before entering the Garden of Gethsemane, the Savior taught, "Verily, verily, I say unto you, He that receiveth whomsoever I send receiveth me; and he that receiveth me receiveth him that sent me" (John 13:20).

In the same opening section of the Doctrine and Covenants, wherein the Lord acknowledged the weaknesses of His servants, He also stated, "What I the Lord have spoken, I have spoken, and I excuse not myself; and though the heavens and the earth pass away, my word shall not pass away, but shall all be fulfilled, whether by mine own voice or by the voice of my servants, it is the same" (Doctrine and Covenants 1:38).

The Lord taught Moses, "I will raise them up a Prophet, . . . like unto thee, and will put my words in his mouth; and he shall speak unto them all that I shall command him. And it shall come to pass, that whosoever will not hearken unto my words which he shall speak in my name, I will require it of him" (Deuteronomy 18:18–19).

Receiving Christ requires that we also receive His servants. We cannot accept Christ while rejecting those He has called to serve. This truth places a certain responsibility on us as members of the Lord's Church. Because we know that the Lord's servants are not perfect, perhaps the greatest challenge for many of us is that when certain policies, procedures, decisions, or statements are given by Church leaders, we will wonder whether those things represent the mind and will of the Lord or the mind and will of imperfect men and women. And when those policies, procedures, decisions, or statements touch a personal nerve or run contrary to our own imperfect mind and will, then our faith can be tested.

Of course, not everything Church leaders say and do represents the will of the Lord. These men and women sometimes express their personal opinions. They have their own personal lives and families and their own mortal growth experience to pass through. But when one of the Lord's servants speaks or acts in the name of the Lord, the responsibility falls on us to seek the witness of the Holy Ghost and follow that guidance.

President Brigham Young taught, "Let every man and woman know, by the whispering of the Spirit of God to themselves, whether their leaders are walking in the path the lord dictates. . . . Let every person be fervent in prayer, until they know the things of God for themselves and become certain that they are walking in the path that leads to everlasting life."[12]

Each of us has a responsibility to seek the witness of the Holy Ghost regarding the direction given through the Lord's servants. It is by divine design that we must each individually look to the Savior to obtain that witness. This mortal testing of faith is deliberate and essential to our Heavenly Father's plan for us. This divinely inspired pattern is meant to focus our attention and faith on Christ, turning away from relying on the arm of flesh, including our own.

In those moments when our faith in following the Lord's prophets is tested, we can recognize this as a divinely planned opportunity to turn our attention to Christ. We can ask the Lord to help us trust in His promises and His ability to accomplish His work. We can ask Him to help us recognize if our perspective is the one that needs changing. We can choose to exercise effort to align our own will to the Lord's will. We can choose to increase our sensitivity to the Holy Ghost. We can strive to better recognize the Savior acting through His servants in mercy.

If I were to paraphrase Moroni's plea in my own words, I think it would go something like this: "We've done the best we know how. We know the writing isn't good enough. We know there may be mistakes. We know we're not perfect. But please don't let our weaknesses stop you from coming unto Christ. Please don't let our failings cause you to doubt the divinity of the work. Please remember that throughout all human history, from the days of Adam, the Lord has been merciful enough to call upon mortals to accomplish His work. Please don't

12. "Remarks By President Brigham Young, Tabernacle, January 19, 1862," *Deseret News*, Feb. 12, 1862, 1.

reject Christ and His gospel just because we aren't ideal messengers. Try to see past our shortcomings and see Christ working through us. Let our weaknesses strengthen your faith in Christ. He is perfect, and His grace is sufficient to compensate for our imperfections."

How merciful has the Lord been? From the days of Adam, He has given us prophets to speak on His behalf. He worked through men like Adam, Enoch, Noah, Abraham, Moses, Isaiah and John the Baptist. He works countless miracles in our lives each day. He sent His Son to rescue us from sin and grief and pain. He appeared to the boy Joseph to usher in the Restoration of the gospel in the last days. The calling of the Prophet Joseph Smith, the restoration of the priesthood, the coming forth of the Book of Mormon, and continuing revelation through living prophets today are all part of God's continuing mercy toward the children of men.

In the previous chapter, we talked about personally experiencing God's mercy in our own lives. Once we've experienced the Savior's redeeming mercy for us, we are able to see more clearly all of God's works through the lens of His mercy. It becomes so much easier to allow that same mercy for others, especially His chosen servants as they also struggle to be perfected in Christ. Remembering that mercy, as Moroni suggests, will be required of each of us as we seek a witness from the Holy Ghost regarding the divinity of this work and a sure testimony of the restored gospel.

Exercises

Ponder the following questions and write down your thoughts.

- Consider the Savior's words in the following verses: Matthew 10:20; Luke 9:48; Luke 10:16; Doctrine and Covenants 84:35–38. What do you learn from these verses?
- Consider the dialogue between Moroni and the Lord as found in Ether 12:23–29. How does the Lord's ability to make weak things become strong apply as it relates to His calling imperfect men and women to do His work?
- Why do you believe the Lord permits imperfection within His Church?

- What can you do to understand and develop the mercy that God has as you observe possible imperfections in the Lord's servants?
- What experiences have you had when your fear of the imperfections of other Church members or leaders caused you to question your testimony? For each of those experiences, consider asking Heavenly Father to teach you how He views that experience and how He views the other individuals involved. Consider asking the Lord, "Can you teach me how I should think and feel about this experience?" Write down the answers you receive.

PRINCIPLE 3: CONVERT DOUBTS INTO SINCERE QUESTIONS

"At length I came to the conclusion that I must either remain in darkness and confusion, or else I must do as James directs, that is, ask of God." (Joseph Smith—History 1:13)

"I DON'T SEE HOW IT MAKES ANY SENSE FOR ME TO PAY TITHING WHEN I can barely pay my rent!"

My friendship with the wonderful sister who voiced this concern allowed her to express her feelings freely. She had been through many significant trials in her life, several of them financial. Now she was working to prepare herself to enter the temple and receive her own temple ordinances.

The Lord's requirements to enter His temples seem to be almost designed to test and develop our faith and trust in Him according to our individual weaknesses. For some Church members, living the law of chastity may be a formidable challenge. For others, it may be the Word of Wisdom that stretches them, or honesty, or sustaining Church leaders. The Lord seems to be able to find that one area for each of us that really tests us to give up our will and demonstrate our faith in Him. For this sister, that challenge came from the Lord's law of tithing.

As we visited that day, we discussed the promises the Lord makes to faithful tithe payers. We studied His words regarding the law of tithing in the book of Malachi (see Malachi 3:8–11). We looked at her finances and how she could make things work to accommodate paying an honest tithe. As her bishop, I had offered to provide assistance with things like groceries and other needs so that she could pay her tithing and receive the Lord's promised blessings for living this law until she could manage on her own. I suggested that the Lord could bless her in ways neither of us could foresee. But none of that justification seemed to provide her what she needed to move forward. None of my feeble attempts to encourage her faith were addressing her real concerns. The finances weren't the real hang-up for her.

At the core of her hesitations were doubt and fear. "How do I know the Lord won't abandon me?" she asked. "How do I know He won't leave me poor and destitute in retirement? The Church has enough money—why does it need mine?" These were some of the concerns she expressed. The principle of paying tithing and its financial implications acted as a trigger for her underlying fears. That fear exposed her doubt about the Lord's desire, ability, and promise to bless her. Her fear also caused her to have subtle doubts about the Church in asking its members to live the law of tithing. It was easier to entertain the belief that she was an exception, or that the commandment was invalid or man-made, than to commit to living it. She was stuck and unable to move forward.

I finally received some desperately needed inspiration. "You know, I don't think you should have to just take my word on this," I said. "You have several concerns. Are you willing to ask the Lord?"

"Ask Him if I should pay my tithing?" she asked.

"No," I responded. "Ask Him about the things you're concerned about."

"What do you mean?"

"Well," I continued, "I don't think the Lord expects you to take this on blind faith. For example, you mentioned you don't see how it makes sense to pay your tithing when you're barely getting by. Can you turn that into a question that you can ask the Lord?"

As we talked, we identified several questions she could ponder herself and take to the Lord:

- "Why does the Church ask me to live this law despite my financial situation?"
- "I'm barely getting by now. How is paying my tithing going to help?"
- "Are you going to abandon me financially if I pay my tithing?"
- "Is this principle from heaven or from men?"
- "Do you want me to pay my tithing? Why?"

I believe it was intriguing to her and somewhat comforting to consider having her real concerns and fears addressed, as opposed to just taking a blind leap of faith or accepting something she didn't understand. When she left the office, I wasn't quite sure if she would actually go to the Lord with her concerns and questions. But I did a fair amount of praying for her, knowing she needed the blessings of paying tithing and the blessings of the temple in her life.

Within a week or so, I received a message from this sister that read, "I paid my tithing and will commit to paying it . . . so I can get my temple recommend along with other blessings of course. :)"

I was so grateful to receive that message. What changed for this sister? In retrospect, I believe that this simple step—moving from a mindset of doubt and fear to a mindset of pondering, and asking sincere questions about her real concerns—opened her heart and mind to receive the revelation, comfort, and strength from heaven that she needed. With this, she was able to get unstuck and move forward in faith.

Of course, this sister still had questions and worries. Very rarely do any of us arrive at a point where all our questions are answered and we no longer need to walk by faith. But great blessings unfolded in this sister's life over the following months and years as she continued to live the law of tithing and participate in temple ordinances. The Lord guided her through subsequent important life, career, and financial decisions, which she was able to make with greater peace and confidence. She is thriving in the gospel today as she waits on the Lord for answers to some of her questions.

We've discussed that looking to Christ in every thought to receive an enduring witness of the restored gospel requires revelation from heaven through the Holy Ghost—that an intellectual witness alone is insufficient. We've also learned that remembering God's mercy for His children, including ourselves, is an essential part of preparing our hearts to receive that witness. Now we consider a third principle: we can choose to act in faith by replacing doubts with sincere, seeking questions.

Converting doubts into questions is a concrete act of faith any Church member can take regardless of the current strength of their testimony. We do this by identifying the true source of our doubts, identifying our underlying fears, and then identifying the sincere questions we long to have answered.

Before we put this process into practice, let's briefly take a closer look at doubt and why the Savior asks us to actively exercise our agency to avoid doubt.

Doubt Not, Fear Not

Immediately following the Savior's counsel to Joseph and Oliver to "look unto [Him] in every thought," He gave this important command: "Doubt not, fear not" (Doctrine and Covenants 6:36).

The scriptures contain many other examples of where the Savior or His servants encouraged God's children to avoid doubt and fear and instead choose faith and belief.

To Jairus, who sought a miracle for his dying daughter, Jesus encouraged, "Be not afraid, only believe" (Mark 5:36).

To the desperate father of the young man possessed with a dumb spirit, Jesus said, "If thou canst believe, all things are possible to him that believeth" (Mark 9:23).

In the Sermon on the Mount, the Savior counseled His disciples, "Neither be ye of doubtful mind" (Luke 12:29).

Jesus promised His disciples that they could command mountains to move, saying, "If ye have faith, and doubt not" (Matthew 21:21).

To all who seek a witness of the truthfulness of His words, the Savior promised, "Whosoever shall believe in my name, doubting nothing, unto him will I confirm all my words, even unto the ends of the earth" (Mormon 9:25).

And the prophet Moroni implored, "Doubt not, but be believing" (Mormon 9:27).

In many of these instances, the Savior recognized an individual's personal struggle with doubt, and their decision to act in faith was necessary before He could provide a desperately needed miracle in their life.

Why does the Lord counsel us to "doubt not"? What is it about doubt that's so harmful? Surely the Lord doesn't expect us to accept everything on blind belief, right? After all, isn't it good to question things?

It's important to note that the word *question* and the word *doubt*, as we find them used in the scriptures, are not the same thing. In fact, they're hardly even related.

Doubt Limits Growth

The modern English word *question* is derived from the Latin word *quaerere*, which means "to seek" or "to ask." Those who speak Spanish or other Latin-derived languages may recognize the continued use today of the Latin derivative word *querer*, which is used to express want, desire, or longing. In English we still use the derivative words *query* and *inquire*. A question is a statement meant to signal a sincere desire to obtain and integrate information.

In contrast, the word *doubt* as used in scripture is defined in the dictionary using terms such as distrust, disbelief, skepticism, suspicion, and fear.[13] It is this expression of doubt that the Savior commands us to actively put aside. Distrust, disbelief, skepticism, and fear are defensive behaviors that limit our ability to receive new knowledge or form trusting relationships. Most of us demonstrate these behaviors when we encounter information or situations we don't yet know how to respond to constructively because of our own lack of knowledge, confidence, or capability. Doubt is a "natural man" response (see Mosiah 3:19).

Doubt, unlike a sincere question, does not allow for discovery or examination. It does not open the mind and heart to learning. Instead, doubt presupposes a conclusion, usually borne out of our own bias or insecurities.

---

13. *Merriam-Webster.com Dictionary*, s.v. "doubt," accessed Oct. 23, 2023, https://www.merriam-webster.com/dictionary/doubt.

You can imagine that it is difficult to form a trusting relationship with God, listen to the words of living prophets, or receive a witness of the Holy Ghost if we are filled with distrust, disbelief, skepticism, or fear. As we grow and mature spiritually, we gradually learn to replace doubt and fear with other constructive behaviors, including confidence and trust in God.

Doubt Causes Us to Mistrust Others

Doubt, because it is defensive and grounded in fear, tends to pit us against God and our fellow brothers and sisters. While sincere questions can open our hearts to understanding the thoughts and motives of others, doubt usually causes us to presume the very worst about others. When we doubt, we often suspect someone is trying to deceive or take advantage of us. We might think or say things about others that we would never dare do if we knew them personally.

For example, to doubt the authenticity of the Book of Mormon, we really have to assume the very worst about Joseph and Emma Smith, Oliver Cowdery, Martin Harris, the Whitmer family, and the many other early Saints who gave so much to bring it forth and who've borne witness of its truthfulness. Doubt would have us question the character of these individuals and suspect they were either delusional, deceived, or intentionally seeking to deceive others.

As another example, the topic of the practice of plural marriage among early Church members has been a challenge of faith for many Latter-day Saints. Our default response to this topic may be to assume the very worst about the motives and intents of Church members who participated in plural marriage. But when we approach the subject with a desire to understand, we are able to consider these individuals and events from different perspectives. We begin to develop empathy for the early Saints who struggled to live a law they believed in, and our hearts open to seeing things through their eyes.

And as a final example, many individuals struggle to accept Christ's atoning power in their lives. When we doubt Christ's ability to change us and cleanse us from sin, we imply that we believe He cannot do what He claims—that His power is somehow limited. Such doubt also suggests that the millions of people who've been transformed through His Atonement are confused or deceptive.

Thus, doubt creates enmity between us and our fellow men and God by causing us to mistrust the motives and intents of others for fear of being deceived.

Doubt Displaces Faith

Perhaps the most significant motivation for Christ's commandment to avoid doubt is captured in this statement by President Thomas S. Monson: "Remember that faith and doubt cannot exist in the same mind at the same time, for one will dispel the other."[14]

Faith is essential to obtaining any and all blessings. Faith motivates all our actions toward promised outcomes. It motivates us to study the scriptures, to pray, to keep the commandments, to repent of our sins, and to seek to know Christ and have His Atonement work in our lives. Without that motivating power of faith, we remain frozen in inaction.

Let's consider a possible definition of faith that may help explain why faith is so essential: "Faith is the principle of belief coupled with action sufficient to obtain a promised result."

One of my favorite illustrations of this is the analogy of a farmer. A farmer may believe that planting his field with seeds and tending it accordingly will yield crops. His fellow farmers may bear witness of this fact. The farmer himself may have seen the process of planting, tending, and harvesting repeatedly throughout his own life. However, while the farmer may know that planting will yield crops, unless the farmer actually puts forth the effort to plant and tend the field, there will be no harvest. Faith is that power that motivates the farmer to put his belief into action, which then enables him to receive the result: a harvest.

Doubt displaces faith by causing us to expend unproductive energy that might otherwise be spent acting in faith. A doubting farmer might spend all his time telling his fellow farmers there is no reason to plant crops; he's certainly not going to spend the energy to plant his own. The result is a season with no harvest.

Similarly, our doubts can prevent us from acting in faith in ways that would draw us to the Savior and provide opportunities for the

---

14. Thomas S. Monson. "Be an Example and a Light," *Ensign*, Nov. 2015, 87.

Holy Ghost to bear witness of truth to our hearts. Doubt can displace the motivation to search the scriptures, seek answers from our Heavenly Father through prayer, live the gospel, make and keep sacred covenants, or repent of our sins. Doubt pushes out the faith that's required to motivate us to act in these productive ways that qualify us to receive revelation and draw us closer to Christ.

These are just a few brief reasons why the Lord consistently encourages us to actively avoid doubt and instead choose faith. While doubt itself is something we all may experience, if not dealt with in healthy ways, doubt will limit our ability to receive new information, to consider new opportunities and ideas, to form and maintain loving relationships with God and others, and to receive revelation from heaven. As the Lord counsels us, doubt is not a place where we want to remain. Doubt may be an unavoidable stop along our journey, but it is not a desirable destination.

The Origin of Our Doubts

Our purpose here is not to dwell on the dangers of doubt. The good news is that as we learned from Peter's experience of walking on water, doubt can actually be an excellent precursor to increased faith if we develop the pattern of looking to Christ when we encounter it. Converting doubts into sincere questions is a simple first step in developing that pattern. We can begin this process by doing the work to identify the true source of our doubts.

Identifying our doubts may seem easy on the surface. But as I've talked with friends in the Church, I've learned that the real source of doubt is often a few layers deeper than what we may initially recognize or express.

Doubt and Fear: Best Friends Forever

Recall that Christ counseled Joseph and Oliver to "doubt not" and "fear not" (Doctrine and Covenants 6:36). Doubt is almost always coupled with underlying fear or a lack of faith and confidence in ourselves and in God. This is important to remember as we identify our doubts. Identifying the personal fears associated with our doubts can help us formulate meaningful questions of the soul that we desperately desire to have personally answered by the Lord.

For example, recall the experience of the dear sister that I shared at the beginning of this chapter. She may have expressed her doubt as something like this: "I don't believe that the commandment to pay tithing comes from the Lord," or perhaps "I don't think the Lord expects *me* to pay tithing because of my circumstances." After our discussion, however, it became apparent that the true source of her doubts was a fear that she would not be financially secure if she lived the law of tithing. Her doubts were also rooted in fear regarding her relationship with the Lord and His willingness and ability to bless her. Until she identified the real sources of her concerns, she could not productively move forward in faith.

For some Church members, the fears that underly doubt may be tied to deeply troubling personal experiences. One sister's faith in the restored gospel was deeply shaken when she learned about the practice of plural marriage among early Church leaders. After discussion, she identified that she had an almost consuming personal fear of her husband becoming unfaithful to her. She had watched the effects of a close family member having broken his marriage covenants with his spouse, leading to the dissolution of their marriage. That personal experience left this sister feeling very unsure about the stability of her own marriage and kept her in a state of fear, always trying to mentally prepare for the worst. The topic of plural marriage acted as a trigger for her personal fears, and she viewed the practice through that lens.

Another sister lived with serious debilitating doubts about God's love for her. She lived in a perpetual state of fear, believing that God judged her daily as to how well she performed to every expectation she placed upon herself. She struggled with debilitating perfectionism. Anything less than a flawless performance in her family life, social life, church service, or other activities meant to her that she was less valuable and less loved. She experienced frequent panic attacks, and her physical health began to suffer. Through our discussion, this sister described having grown up in a home where expectations were high, where love was not expressed verbally or physically, and where approval from her parents seemed conditional on obedience and performance to expectations.

Some Church members have experienced the trauma of sexual, physical, or emotional abuse as children or adults. For these individuals, deeply rooted trauma and fears may manifest themselves as doubt. It is not uncommon for these individuals to experience an inability to feel God's love, doubts about the existence of God, difficulty in accepting the healing power of the Savior's Atonement in their lives, or a fear of men in positions of authority. For these Church members, professional, qualified counseling is almost always essential in their healing process.

These are just a few examples illustrating how our personal experiences and innermost fears can influence our doubts about the restored gospel of Jesus Christ. Though not always the case, doubts may often be a reflection of what we fear most. Although many Church members may express doubts about similar topics, the underlying emotions and fears surrounding doubt are unique and deeply personal and can only be resolved individually.

This reality of the connection between doubt and fear means that the quest to resolve our doubts is far more important than merely receiving a testimony of the Lord's restored Church. When doubt and fear overwhelm us, what's at stake also includes our personal happiness, our ability to experience peace and joy, our ability to reach our potential and bless the lives of others, and our ability to feel God's love for us personally. It is therefore essential that we not run away from our doubts; instead, we need to learn how to look unto Christ in every thought and do the work that will allow Him to heal our wounded souls, wipe away our tears, and replace doubt and fear with faith and confidence.

Common Experiences That May Lead to Doubt

Are you ready to begin identifying your doubts? What elements about the Lord's restored gospel and the Church are you struggling with? What experiences in your life may have sown the initial seeds of doubt for you? The list below includes some of the common expressions of doubt that many Church members experience. It is certainly not comprehensive, but it may help you identify or express your own doubts. You might mark the examples you identify with as you read through them.

- Doubts may arise when we encounter new information about Church history or early Church leaders that differs from our previously held image of the Church. Common examples may include the practice of plural marriage among early Church members and leaders, the former withholding of priesthood ordinations for faithful Black men in the Church, multiple accounts of Joseph Smith's First Vision, or seeming character flaws, statements, or mistakes from early Church leaders.
- Doubts may arise when scientific or historical evidence appears contrary to generally accepted beliefs of the Church or its members. Common examples may include the description of animals found in the Book of Mormon, the origin of the Book of Abraham, the ancestry and DNA of Native Americans, or conflicting scientific information regarding the supposed health benefits of substances discouraged by the Word of Wisdom.
- Doubts may arise when we feel personally offended by the comments or actions of other Church members or leaders such as a bishop, Relief Society president, stake president, or General Authority.
- Doubts may arise when the performance or behavior of Church members falls short of what we expect from the Lord's people.
- Doubts may arise when we feel overlooked for callings or service in the Church.
- Doubts may arise when our own sins or shortcomings seem insurmountable.
- Doubts may arise because we feel that we don't fit in with other Church members or that living the Church's standards is beyond our reach.
- Doubts may arise when a Church policy is difficult for us to understand or accept or when it personally affects us or someone we love. Examples may include the Church's teachings and policies regarding same-sex relationships, standards for

baptism and temple ordination, or questions surrounding the role of women in relation to priesthood offices.

- Doubts may arise when a Church doctrine or policy seemingly puts us at odds with members of our community, peer group, or coworkers.
- Doubts may arise when we are mocked for our beliefs.
- Doubts may present themselves with the onset or persistence of mental illnesses such as depression, anxiety, or diagnosed chemical imbalances.
- Doubts may arise when we grow tired of serving in the Lord's kingdom.
- Doubts may arise when doctrinal prophecies seem delayed or unfulfilled.
- Doubts may arise when temple ordinances seem difficult to understand or enjoy.
- Doubts may arise out of concern about how the Church uses or allocates temporal resources such as tithing, fast offerings, temple funds, ward budgets, investments, or property.
- Doubts may arise when a heartfelt prayer seemingly goes long unanswered.
- Doubts may arise when we encounter a significant life trial such as a job loss, divorce, marital discord, loss of a loved one, or major health problems.
- Doubts may arise when our ability to trust God or others has been compromised by a serious life trauma such as physical, emotional, or sexual abuse.
- Doubts may arise from our inability to feel God's love for us due to mistreatment from others or our own lack of self-love.
- Doubts may arise out of fear that surrendering our lives to the Lord will require sacrifices that we're unwilling to make.

This is obviously not comprehensive—these items are just some of the experiences that may correlate with doubt in our lives. Any life experiences that cause us to lose hope or to be lost in fear, distrust, or anger may trigger doubt in our lives. Each of us has likely had experience with at least some of these. Remember that it is not the experiences themselves that cause us to doubt but how we each uniquely respond to those experiences. Those with the brightest testimonies and strongest faith are often those who have passed through many faith-testing experiences and have learned to look to the Savior in the process.

Act in Faith: Identify Your Doubts and Fears

In the next chapter, we're going to discuss how to formulate sincere questions that we can take to the Lord and ponder ourselves. Before we get there, let's finish this chapter by getting very practical about identifying the doubts we may have.

Consider the following approach:

- Express each doubt in writing. You might use wording such as "I have a hard time accepting _____" or "I struggle to believe that _____" or even "I don't believe that _____."
- Write down any and all underlying fears or emotions that might be associated with each doubt. Try using wording such as "I'm afraid of ______" or "I'm afraid that ______" or "I worry that _____" or "I've been hurt by _____." Try to go as many layers deep into your fears as possible by asking yourself questions such as "Where does this fear come from?" "Why am I afraid of this?" or "What experiences in my life may have contributed to these fears?" This may be a long list, and that's okay. Alternatively, you may not be able to identify any fears associated with your doubt. That's okay too.

Exercises

Ponder the following questions and write down your thoughts.

- Why do you believe the Lord counsels us to avoid doubt and instead choose to act in faith?
- Consider the list of scriptures found in the Topical Guide under the topic "Doubt." What insights do you gain from these verses?

- What personal insights did you receive from going through the action of identifying your own doubts and fears?

Ask and It Shall Be Given You

Having done the work to identify our doubts, we can next identify the sincere questions of our souls. These are questions we can ponder and take to the Lord as we sincerely seek answers from heaven. While the Lord has consistently counseled us to avoid doubt, the scriptures are filled with His pleas for us to come to Him with our sincere questions. There is perhaps no invitation more often repeated in scripture by the Savior or His servants than this: "Ask, and it shall be given you; seek, and ye shall find; knock, and it shall be opened unto you: For every one that asketh receiveth; and he that seeketh findeth; and to him that knocketh it shall be opened" (Matthew 7:7–8).

In my own study of the scriptures, I've marked more than thirty occurrences or variations of that message, and I'm still encountering them.[15] For me, such frequent repetition of this message indicates how desperately our Savior wants us to come to Him and ask for help. Most of those invitations are from the Savior Himself. One of my favorite examples about this subject is found in Doctrine and Covenants as follows: "Ask the Father in my name in faith, believing you shall receive, and you shall have the Holy Ghost, which manifesteth all things which are expedient unto the children of men" (Doctrine and Covenants 18:18).

---

15. See the Exercises section at the end of this chapter for a sample of such verses.

Did you catch that? The Lord promises that He will provide us all the answers we truly need through the Holy Ghost—if we ask in faith.

The Power of Asking Questions

Why is asking sincere questions so essential in our search for truth? Several years ago, a few colleagues from work and I attended a talk entitled "Finding Answers to Life's Greatest Questions" in Menlo Park, California. The guest speaker that evening was Clayton M. Christensen. Elder Christensen, who regrettably passed away during the writing of this book, was a Latter-day Saint, a former Area Seventy, a professor of business at the Harvard Business School, and a very well-known personality and author in the business world. His background and notoriety drew a large and diverse crowd of attendees from the San Francisco Bay area that evening.

In his talk, Brother Christensen related a dream wherein he was permitted to visit heaven and converse with the Lord. The Lord showed Clayton a massive warehouse with shelves filled top to bottom and end to end with truth and knowledge, all of which would be very useful to mankind on earth.

Clayton worked up the courage to ask the Lord a question, which I'll paraphrase. He asked, "Why are you keeping all this knowledge stored here in a warehouse in heaven? Why don't you send it all down to earth so that mankind can benefit from it?"

The Lord indicated that He would love to give this knowledge to us on earth, but there was a problem. In order to illustrate the problem, the Lord pulled a package of truth from one of the shelves and pointed to a man down on earth. "You see that man?" the Lord asked Clayton. "Watch what happens when I try to send this knowledge to him." With that, the Lord threw the package of knowledge from heaven down to the man on earth. But nothing happened. The package went straight through the man, having no effect on him at all.

In discussing this phenomenon with the Lord, Clayton learned that God had a great desire to share all that He has with His children, but unless men and women first have a sincere desire to learn, they are not prepared to receive truth. Sincere questions, he learned, create a receptor in the mind and heart of the inquirer that enables them to receive knowledge from heaven. Without the preparation created by a sincere question, the Lord cannot give them the truth and knowledge they need.[16]

Why are questions so important? By doing the spiritual work to identify, ponder, and ask the right questions, we prepare our own hearts, minds, and character to receive revelation from heaven that our Heavenly Father already wants to give us.

So how do we identify the right questions to ask?

The Right Questions Are Sincere

What is a sincere question? And what does it mean to "ask in faith" (Doctrine and Covenants 18:18) as the Lord counseled?

The Apostle James, in counseling us to ask of God when we need wisdom, also defined what it means to be sincere in our asking. You'll recognize these verses as the same verses that touched the heart of a young Joseph Smith when he desperately sought answers from heaven. He said, "If any of you lack wisdom, let him ask of God, that giveth to all men liberally, and upbraideth not; and it shall be given him. But let him ask in faith, nothing wavering. For he that wavereth is like a wave of the sea driven with the wind and tossed. For let not that man think that he shall receive any thing of the Lord" (James 1:5–7).

Recall the definition of faith suggested in the previous chapter: "Faith is the principle of belief coupled with action sufficient to obtain a promised result." When James counsels us to "ask in faith, nothing wavering," he means that we should ask with the intent to act on the answers we receive.

Our questions should not merely be to satisfy our curiosity. Christ specifically spoke against this when he stated, "Ye ask, and receive not, because ye ask amiss, that ye may consume it upon your lusts" (James 4:3). We must not expect the Lord to reveal truth to us if our intent is to cast it aside. Rather, a sincere question means that we sincerely want to receive and follow the Lord's guidance. Sincere means "with intent to follow."

---

16. Clayton M. Christensen, "Finding Answers to Life's Greatest Questions." Author's notes from Elder Christensen talk given at a Latter-day Saint chapel in Menlo Park, CA, in January 2017.

One of the greatest examples of a sincere question was asked by the Lamanite king to the Book of Mormon missionary Aaron. After Aaron had taught the king the gospel of Jesus Christ and the plan of salvation, the king asked, "What shall I do that I may have this eternal life of which thou hast spoken? Yea, what shall I do that I may be born of God, having this wicked spirit rooted out of my breast, and receive his Spirit, that I may be filled with joy, that I may not be cast off at the last day? Behold, said he, I will give up all that I possess, yea, I will forsake my kingdom, that I may receive this great joy" (Alma 22:15).

Now *that* is a very sincere question. The king had no idea what he needed to do. But he was willing to make great sacrifices to receive the blessing if only he could know how to act.

As we ponder our sincere questions, we should strive to have that same longing—that same desire to really know and do the Lord's will. Are we humble enough to admit that we don't have the answers we seek, and that only the Lord does? Are we willing to acknowledge that we may have been wrong in our thoughts, words, or actions and be willing to correct them? Are we willing to change our position on something if only we can receive needed direction from our Heavenly Father? Are we willing to make changes in our mind, heart, and behavior in response to the answers we receive?

Perhaps that sounds like a tall order. We may be feeling we're not ready for that level of sincere asking. That's okay. Regardless of where we are in our preparedness to sincerely seek revelation, each of us can act in faith today by doing the work to identify our questions.

The Right Questions Are the Ones That Matter Most

As we work to replace doubts with sincere questions, we begin to realize that some questions are more important than others. Our hearts become open to revelation from the Holy Ghost when we focus on the questions that matter most.

Elder Lawrence E. Corbridge gave a talk at BYU as a General Authority Seventy in which he used the terms "Primary Questions" and "Secondary Questions."[17] We can benefit from this simple framework. Primary questions are those questions that, when answered, provide a bedrock foundation for our testimony and relationship with Christ and His restored Church on the earth. When we encounter things we don't understand, the witness of the Holy Ghost that we receive in response to the primary questions can act as a secure anchor for our testimony while we work through secondary questions.

Our most important questions have to do with our relationship with God as our Father, with our witness of Christ and the personal effect of His Atonement in our lives, and with our witness from the Holy Ghost about fundamental principles and events of the Restoration of the gospel in the latter days.

Let me suggest what I think are some of the most important questions that any Church member should prioritize finding answers to. Answers to these questions will help us feel secure in our relationship with our Heavenly Father and Savior and help establish the foundation of our testimony in Christ's restored Church. I'll pose them in an interview style to help make them more personal. I invite you to pause with each question and answer each one sincerely in your heart.

- Do you have a witness through the Holy Ghost that you are a son or daughter of God and that He loves you?
- Have you personally experienced God's love for you in your life?
- Have you experienced the redeeming power of Jesus Christ and His Atonement in your life? Is Christ's Atonement actively working in your life to change you?
- Do you have a witness that the Book of Mormon is what it claims to be—an ancient record of prophets that contains the fulness of the gospel of Jesus Christ that was preserved and brought forth by the power of God?
- Do you have a witness that Joseph Smith was called and ordained of God as His instrument to bring about the Restoration of the Church of Jesus Christ in the latter days?

---

17. Lawrence E. Corbridge, "Stand Forever" (Brigham Young University devotional, Jan. 22, 2019), speeches.byu.edu.

- Do you have a witness that priesthood authority has been restored to the earth and that the keys to administer the gospel and its ordinances continue with the modern-day prophet, First Presidency, and Quorum of the Twelve Apostles of The Church of Jesus Christ of Latter-day Saints?

I list these questions as among the most important because, in my experience, once we receive a witness from the Holy Ghost regarding these truths, we are able to move forward in faith, living the restored gospel of Jesus Christ while we patiently search for answers to our other questions.

Secondary Questions

Obviously there are a lot of questions beyond those I listed as being "primary." It's important we spend time here because, ironically, the secondary questions are those that most frequently pose a stumbling block for many members of the Church. Secondary questions typically arise from a few different themes:

- Teachings, doctrines, or historical events for which the Lord has chosen not to provide fully detailed explanations, thus leaving some ambiguity and allowing for personal discovery, interpretation, discussion, and revelation.
- Church policies, practices, or guidelines that touch on topics that are sensitive in our modern political or social climate.
- Actions or statements by past Church members and leaders that touch on current sensitive political or social topics and are further complicated by imperfect and incomplete historical context.

Some common examples of topics in these categories include questions around same-sex attraction, plural marriage, the Word of Wisdom, personal behaviors or actions of Church leaders and members, historical facts regarding the Book of Mormon, racial issues, priesthood authority, tithing and Church finances, and so on.

Now, it's worth asking: Are these questions unimportant? And the answer is of course not. Indeed, these topics can be very important.

One young woman, through tears, sincerely asked in a group setting what was going to happen to her baby brother who had recently died at birth. Would she see him again? Would her mom have the chance to raise him? Are those sincere, important questions? Oh my goodness, absolutely! Can this young woman come to more personally know her Heavenly Father and the infinite reach of Jesus Christ's Atonement as she searches for answers to these questions? Yes.

What about the young brother or sister who comes to the realization that they experience same-sex attraction and is now going through the wrestle of asking themselves questions such as "How does Heavenly Father feel about me? Where do I fit in the Lord's Church on earth? How will my family members and friends respond to this? What is life going to be like for me?" Are these important, even essential questions? Yes. In such a moment of struggle, those questions can seem existential and can deeply affect the peace and happiness of that precious son or daughter of God.

Indeed, I believe that every sincere question—asked with real intent to draw us closer to God and Christ and truth—is an important question. Perhaps one reason to consider these questions as secondary is that our ability to patiently and faithfully look to Christ as we seek answers to these questions usually comes *after* receiving the fundamental testimony of our relationship to God, of Jesus's role as Savior and Redeemer, and of the Restoration of the gospel.

The precious son or daughter of God grappling with same-sex attraction desperately needs the peace that comes from receiving a personal witness of God's love for them as His child. They need a witness and understanding of our Heavenly Father's loving plan for His children, of Christ's Atonement, and of the great gift of agency we've been given. And if they can find solid grounding in the fundamental truths of the restored gospel, the Holy Ghost can then guide them to the answers they need to know in order to move forward.

Such questions don't have to derail us from living the gospel or cause us to leave the Lord's Church or stray from the counsel of living prophets. We can receive sufficient witness from the Holy Ghost regarding the primary questions to allow us to move forward in faith and live the restored gospel while we continue to seek answers to these important secondary questions.

Another reason to consider these types of questions as secondary is that when we are struggling with our testimony as a result of doubts surrounding these topics, quite often we may be seeking a witness of the primary truths we mentioned above but trying to obtain it indirectly through these secondary topics.

For example, one brother shared significant doubts regarding the Church's policies around the Word of Wisdom. The doubts were significant enough to cause him to leave the Church. As we talked, it became evident he was really struggling with doubts about his relationship with the Savior, mistrust of priesthood leadership from past troubling experiences, and a witness of modern-day prophets and priesthood authority. The Word of Wisdom provided a platform for his doubts, but it was not the primary problem. If he could solidify his witness of those primary questions, he would be able to faithfully move forward until the Lord could answer his questions regarding the Word of Wisdom.

In reality, if we allow secondary questions to prevent us from accepting and living the gospel, we will be forever stuck. That's because the number of secondary questions is infinite. There is always more to know about any given gospel topic or curiosity. There is always more that the Lord has not yet explained or revealed. There are always more questions about history than there are available historical details. There will always be more questions in this life than there are answers. If we waited for these answers before acting in faith on what we do know, we would not progress. Too many Church members remain stuck here, looking for answers to secondary questions but not able to exercise the faith that would ultimately lead to those answers.

I believe that the Lord will help us find answers to any sincere question, and if these secondary issues are currently limiting our ability to move forward in faith, we absolutely should be asking them. But as we identify our sincere questions, it's worth asking ourselves, "Is this really my most important question? Or am I really longing for a witness from heaven about the fundamental truths of the gospel and this is getting in my way?" If you determine that your question is really a secondary question, don't erase it, but consider whether there is a primary question at the heart of your concerns—a primary question that, if answered, would give you the faith and strength to carry forward while you seek answers to your secondary questions.

Does It Matter?

One day, while serving as a bishop, I received a text message from a dear sister indicating that she was leaving the Church. She'd recently learned things she hadn't previously known about Joseph Smith and the subject of plural marriage. She thanked me for all the help I'd given her in the past but indicated it was all just too much for her. She wasn't prepared to talk about things at that time, but I told her I understood how challenging this was and let her know that if she ever felt like she wanted to talk, my door was wide open and I would be there for her.

In the ensuing months I'd occasionally hear from her. Her husband was a member of another faith, and she began attending his church. But over time, she started to feel a pull back to the restored gospel. She'd had an underlying testimony of the primary truths of the gospel, including a witness of the Book of Mormon. She'd had a lifetime of experiences at church that added to her testimony. She had made covenants in the temple and had some special experiences there. And the Savior had performed miracles in her life. But she was stuck on the subject of plural marriage and did not know how to move forward.

Finally, one day, she unexpectedly messaged me and asked if she could come talk. As we met in the office, I listened while she shared her feelings. As her bishop, I felt that my role was not to give her the answers but to help her discover how to find them for herself with the help of the Holy Ghost. When she finished, I felt prompted to help her make a sort of decision flowchart—one of those diagrams where at every question you take a different branch in the chart depending on the yes or no answer, which leads to the next question and eventually a decision or action.

I grabbed a marker and started drawing on the whiteboard. We started out asking a single question. And for every question we asked, we put down the possible answers of yes, no, and maybe (or I don't know). And each one of those answers then led to another question or decision. We attempted to take a fearless, unbiased approach of deciding what each yes, no, or maybe answer would lead to and not shying away from tough questions.

I won't try to recreate that flowchart here or list out all the hypothetical questions she considered, but here are a few:

- Has the Lord ever commanded or allowed plural marriage?
- Did the Lord condone plural marriage as practiced by Abraham, Isaac, and Jacob in the Old Testament?
    - If not, did this disqualify them as the Lord's people?
    - If yes, what would we learn from this? Why would the Lord condone or command such a practice?
- Did the Lord command Joseph Smith to practice plural marriage?
    - If not, would this disqualify Joseph as a prophet?
    - If not, would this invalidate the Book of Mormon or the restoration of the priesthood?
    - If so, did Joseph get it all correct? Did he make any mistakes?
- Were Brigham Young and the later Saints commanded to implement plural marriage?
    - If not, does this invalidate the restored gospel?
    - If so, why did the Lord command the Saints to end plural marriage?

Aside from yes/no questions like these, this exercise allowed her to fearlessly consider other difficult hypothetical questions such as the following: "How did Church members feel about this?" "What would have happened if Church members hadn't done this?" "What would happen if Church members were asked to live this again today?" "Sexuality aside, what other factors might motivate plural marriage?" "What about societies that practice plural marriage today?" "What is the extent of God's mercy toward His children and His church on this subject?" Difficult, complex questions.

After about half an hour of discussion, this wonderful sister looked at me and said, "I've never thought about it this way before." She sat there for a few moments and finally said, "Maybe it's not important."

"Huh?" I thought. After all, I'd just spent thirty minutes on this exercise and was pretty pleased with what we'd produced.

She explained that while she'd like to know the concrete answers to all these questions, maybe they weren't so important. She already knew that the Book of Mormon was true. She'd had a witness of the Restoration of the gospel through the Prophet Joseph Smith. And most importantly, she knew what she had felt and experienced at church. "So," she said, "maybe this isn't so important."

Now, let me acknowledge that each of us might go through that analysis and have a very different set of questions, decisions, and outcomes. I don't expect anyone to come to the same conclusion as this sister—and she still has a lot of unanswered questions. The point is that she went through the rigor of evaluating the topic fearlessly from every angle and considering what the outcome would mean based on the possible answers. That process allowed her to confront her fears openly and focus in on what mattered most to her, and it allowed for the Spirit to give her the personal revelation that she needed to move forward.

So as we ponder our questions, it's worth asking ourselves what the potential answers will mean and what our next questions and actions would be if we knew the answer. Doing so may help us to identify which questions really matter to us and which ones don't.

Regarding the relative importance of some questions versus others, Elder Tad R. Callister stated:

> I can live with some human imperfections, even among prophets of God—that is to be expected in mortal beings. I can live with some alleged scientific findings contrary to the Book of Mormon; time will correct those. And I can live with some seeming historical anomalies; they are minor in the total landscape of truth. But I cannot live without the doctrinal truths and ordinances restored by Joseph Smith, I cannot live without the priesthood of God to bless my family, and I cannot live without knowing my wife and children are sealed to me for eternity. That is the choice we face—a few unanswered questions on one hand versus a host of doctrinal

certainties and the power of God on the other. And for me, and I hope for you, the choice is an easy one and a rational one.[18]

Questions to Consider

In this chapter, we've remembered the Savior's frequent and sincere plea for us to come to Him with sincere questions. We've learned that sincere questions have the power to prepare our hearts and minds to receive revelation and new information. We've learned that the right questions are asked with real intent to act on the answers. We've discussed that the questions that matter most are those that provide a witness of the fundamental truths of the restored gospel and our relationship with God.

Are you ready to begin to identify your questions? Below is a list of example questions that might help you formulate your own sincere questions. The list is not comprehensive. As you read through them, consider marking those that resonate with you.

- Am I a child of God?
- Heavenly Father, do You love me? Can You help me to feel Your love for me?
- Can I be forgiven of my sins?
- Have I been forgiven of my sins?
- Does Jesus's Atonement apply to me?
- Did Jesus Christ suffer for me and my sins?
- Can You help me to change?
- What do I need to change?
- How can I overcome this addiction?
- Did Heavenly Father and His Son, Jesus Christ, appear to Joseph Smith?
- Is the Book of Mormon true?
- How can I obtain a witness of the Book of Mormon?
- Have I obtained a witness of the Book of Mormon?

---

18. Tad R. Callister, "What Is the Blueprint of Christ's Church?" (Church Educational System fireside for young adults, Jan. 12, 2014), broadcasts.ChurchofJesusChrist.org.

- Was Joseph Smith a true prophet?
- Does Christ lead the Church today?
- Are the First Presidency and the Quorum of the Twelve Apostles really true prophets, seers, and revelators called of God?
- Why do we need the Church today?
- Why was I not asked to serve in this calling?
- Why did Joseph Smith and other early Church leaders institute and practice plural marriage?
- Can you help me understand why the early Saints felt so strongly about plural marriage?
- Why have Church leaders felt to establish such a strong position regarding marriage as defined between a man and a woman?
- Why have Church leaders felt it necessary to establish policies around same-sex marriage?
- Where do I fit into the Church or kingdom of God if I experience same-sex attraction?
- Why are women presently not ordained to the priesthood?
- What is the role of women in the kingdom of God?
- What is the role of men in the kingdom of God?
- Are men and women's roles intended to be different, or is this something temporary?
- How does God view women?
- What is the role of Heavenly Mother?
- Why did it take so long for Black people to be allowed to receive the priesthood?
- Why does the Church teach and require living the Word of Wisdom to be baptized and receive a temple recommend?
- Why do some historical evidences seem to contradict Book of Mormon history?
- How can I gain a witness of the law of tithing?
- How should I feel about the Church's use of tithing and other funds?
- Why did this difficult experience happen to me in my life when I've tried to live the gospel?

- Can I ever be healed from the effects of abuse I've experienced in my life?
- How can I forgive what this person has done to me? Why should I forgive?
- How should I deal with this experience with a ward member who offended me?
- How should I feel about this experience with my priesthood leader who offended me?
- Where can I look for answers to my questions?
- Who can I talk to for help with what I'm struggling with?
- How can I come to know my Savior better?
- Can you teach me how to think about this topic?
- Can you teach me how to feel about this topic?

These are merely some examples. Hopefully this list helps you think about the questions that matter most to you.

Act in Faith: Identify Your Sincere Questions

You may consider building on the exercise we started in the last chapter where we identified our doubts and underlying fears in writing. We can now add our sincere questions.

- Review: Express each doubt in writing.
- Review: Write down any and all underlying fears that might be associated with each doubt.
- Act: For each identified doubt or fear, write down the sincere questions of your soul that you would like to ponder and ask the Lord.

Remember, even though many people may express doubts about the same subject, our doubts, fears, and questions are uniquely personal. Hopefully you've already felt the guidance of the Holy Ghost as you've done the work to identify your own doubts, fears, and questions. The Spirit always accompanies us when we act in faith.

I again give my witness that whatever doubts we may have, or however weak we may feel our testimony of the gospel currently is, each of us can exercise faith in Christ today and accept His plea to "doubt not" and "fear not" by choosing to exchange our doubts for sincere, seeking questions. Identifying the sincere questions that matter most to our souls will turn our hearts to the Savior and prepare us to receive revelation through the Holy Ghost.

Exercises

Ponder the following questions and write down your thoughts.

- What did you gain by going through the action of identifying and writing down your doubts, fears, and sincere questions?
- Consider the following verses regarding the Savior's promise of "ask and it shall be given unto you." Write down your feelings about what you've read. Matthew 7:7–8; 18:19–20; 21:22; Mark 11:23–24; John 14:13–14; 15:7; 16:23–24; James 1:5–6; 1 John 5:14–15; Jeremiah 29:12–13; 1 Nephi 8:11; 2 Nephi 4:35; 32:4; Enos 1:15; 3 Nephi 14:7–8; 17:3; 27:9; 27:28–29; Mormon 9:21; Ether 3:2; Moroni 7:26; Doctrine and Covenants 4:7; 8:1; 10:21; 18:18; 42:3; 42:61; 42:68; 46:7; 46:30; 50:29; 66:9; 88:63–65; 101:27.
- Consider using one of your questions to create a decision diagram, as described in this chapter regarding one sister's struggle with the subject of plural marriage. For each question, ask yourself what the next question or action would be if the answer to your question were hypothetically yes, no, or "I don't know." Continue the diagram until you have exhausted all follow-up questions. Consider how you feel and what the Holy Ghost is trying to teach you as you consider each possible answer or outcome.

Principle 4: Hold Tight to What You Already Know

"I know that [God] loveth his children; nevertheless, I do not know the meaning of all things." (1 Nephi 11:17)

I was enjoying my quiet, solitary drive from San Jose to our stake Young Women's camp. It was held each summer at the breathtakingly beautiful Camp Ritchie located on a pristine lake in the mountains of Pioneer, California. As a bishop, I had the privilege of being invited each year for the final day of camp to spend time with the young women and to host an evening devotional with the youth and leaders from our ward. Perhaps the real motivation for the invitation was that my services would then be employed in a late-night cleaning of the camp lodge and shuttling girls back home the next day. Over the years I came to feel that Young Women's camp was one of the most sacred places on earth. My three-hour drive each year to camp gave me opportunity to quietly ponder and seek guidance from the Holy Ghost about what to discuss with the young women in our ward devotional.

The girls had spent the week doing all kinds of exciting activities, including archery, hiking, boating, water skiing, rock climbing, rappelling, and arts and crafts; spiritual activities that included daily scripture study and devotionals; and the typical rambunctious fun of camp songs, dances, skits, and late-night chats with the girls in their cabins. But at our ward devotional, when I asked my young women what their favorite part of camp had been that year, they unanimously agreed that the devotional with our stake president and his wife was the highlight.

The evening prior to my arrival, our stake president and his wife held a camp-wide devotional where they discussed questions that the young women had anonymously written and submitted throughout the week. Those questions were sincere. Some of them touched on difficult topics we've already mentioned in this book. Many of them revealed deep, personal fears and life struggles that these wonderful daughters of God were experiencing in their lives. As the girls shared their experience with me, it was clear they had felt God's love for them as the stake president and his wife expressed their love and followed the Spirit in discussing their sincere questions. As the girls shared their thoughts, I felt I knew what message to discuss with them that evening.

Brother Brad Wilcox once gave a talk to the youth of the Church entitled "Filling Your Testimony Tank."[19] In this talk, he suggested that we often incorrectly think about a testimony of the gospel using "light switch terminology." We sometimes talk about a testimony as something that is either on or off—something that we either have or don't have, or something we find and then lose and then find again. Brother Wilcox suggested to the youth that a much better analogy for a testimony is a gas tank, like you would find in a car. Between the two extremes of completely empty and completely full, there are an infinite number of points where the tank is partially full.

I shared Brother Wilcox's analogy with my young women. As we enjoyed the breathtaking view of the lake from our coveted overlook on Inspiration Point, I handed out papers and pencils and asked the girls and their leaders to draw the outline of a gas tank around the edge of the paper.

"Now," I said, "starting at the bottom of the tank, let's start filling our tank from the bottom up by writing down two things. First, write down truths that you know about the gospel. These are things

---

19. Brad Wilcox, *Filling Your Testimony Tank* (Salt Lake City, UT: Deseret Book, 2015), audio CD.

you've personally received a witness of from the Holy Ghost that you feel to be true. And second, write down any spiritual experiences you remember when you've felt the Holy Ghost or God's love for you."

As the young women wrote, I noticed them writing things such as "I know God loves me," "I know Jesus died for me," "I know the Book of Mormon is true," and "I know we're all children of God."

The girls also wrote personal spiritual experiences that started with things like "When my grandmother died . . ." "When I visited Nauvoo . . ." "When we moved here . . ." "When I was in seminary . . ." and "When I was reading the Book of Mormon . . ."

I noticed they all had a different number of things written down. I also noticed that none of their tanks were empty.

When we finished, I asked if the girls wanted to share anything they'd written, and a few did. This sharing sparked some moments of "Oh yeah—I could write that one too" from some of the other girls.

After sharing, I began to ask a few questions.

"Does anyone have a completely full tank?"

Nobody did.

"Do any of you have a completely empty tank?"

Again, nobody did.

"So what about all that space left over in our tanks? What does that space represent?" We talked about how that space represents all the things they don't yet know, which is actually a lot.

"So," I asked, "just because the tank has a bunch of empty space in it, does that mean the fuel in the tank isn't good?"

"No," they responded.

I then joked with one of the girls: "Jenni, if I handed you the keys to my car today and said, 'Take it—it's yours. Happy birthday. Treat 'er nice,' would you take it?"

"Absolutely!" she responded.

"Now, what if I said, 'Oh, but Jenni—I should probably tell you that it's only got a quarter tank of gas in it'? How many of you girls would say, 'Oh, you know what? It's okay, never mind—I'll just find another car with a full tank'?"

They unanimously agreed that would be crazy.

"Of course," I said. "In fact, if you've got a car that's low on fuel, what's the first thing you're going to use the gas in the tank for?"

"To go get more gas," they responded.

"Exactly. We use the fuel that we do have in the tank to get us to a place where we can fill up the tank."

We talked about how this makes perfect sense when we talk about fuel in our cars, but many people leave the Church because of the things they don't know, and they forget about the things that they do know.

I then asked the girls to draw a line in their tank above what they'd written and to fill the rest of their tank with their sincere questions about the gospel—with the things they did not yet know but wanted to know.

"Now," I asked, "do the things you don't yet know mean more to you than what you do already know? Would you give up the truths you know and the spiritual experiences you've had because of the part of the tank you haven't filled yet?"

We finished the meeting discussing some of their sincere questions and talking about how they could use what they already know to help them find answers to the things they don't yet know. I bore my testimony of the things I did know to be true. I expressed my confidence in them and my witness that they already knew a lot and had strong testimonies of faith. I bore my witness that God loved them and would continue to bless them with a growing witness of truth through the Holy Ghost as they continued to live the gospel.

What Greater Witness Can You Have than from God?

One of the most important things we can all do when wading through a trial of our faith is to remember and hold on fiercely to the witnesses of truth God has already given us. The spiritual experiences we have had—those truths the Holy Ghost has burned into our hearts—can act as a reliable life preserver if we suddenly find ourselves lost on a sea of doubt and questions.

Before Oliver Cowdery ever met Joseph Smith, he received a witness from God that the work of the Restoration was true and that he had a role to play in it. Oliver had learned about Joseph's experiences and the gold plates while lodging in the home of Joseph's parents in Manchester. Over many months the subject increasingly pressed upon

Oliver's mind, and he told the Smiths he was convinced that he should travel to Harmony where Joseph and Emma were living and assist in the work of translating. "I have made it a subject of prayer," Oliver said, "and I firmly believe that it is the will of the Lord that I should go and there is a work for me to do in this thing and I am determined if there is to attend to it."[20] The Smiths encouraged Oliver to seek a testimony for himself of the validity of the work, which he privately did.

In April 1829, Oliver, accompanied by Joseph's brother Samuel Smith, made the more than 100-mile journey through cold, snow, rain, and mud to the home of Joseph and Emma in Harmony. Upon meeting Joseph for this first time, Joseph informed Oliver that he'd been expecting him and that the Lord had told Joseph He would send him a scribe to assist in the work of translation.

One might think that these experiences alone could serve as an unwavering witness for Oliver. But as we have learned, even the most faithful are not exempt from moments of doubt. Soon after beginning to help Joseph with the translation, Oliver began to question whether the work he was engaged in was true. He asked Joseph if he would seek a revelation from the Lord on his behalf. That revelation is now found in section 6 of the Doctrine and Covenants, and the counsel the Lord gave to Oliver there is loving, precious, and very applicable to each of us today. The Lord told Oliver:

> Behold, thou knowest that thou hast inquired of me and I did enlighten thy mind; and now I tell thee these things that thou mayest know that thou hast been enlightened by the Spirit of truth. . . .
>
> Verily, verily, I say unto you, if you desire a further witness, cast your mind upon the night that you cried unto me in your heart, that you might know concerning the truth of these things.
>
> Did I not speak peace to your mind concerning the matter? What greater witness can you have than from God? (Doctrine and Covenants 6:15, 22–23)

---

20. Lucy Mack Smith, History, 1844–1845, book 8, page 1, josephsmithpapers.org.

When faithful Oliver encountered doubt, the Lord counseled him to look back and to remember and hold on to the witness he'd already received. And he reestablished that witness by confirming to Oliver that it was indeed from the Holy Ghost.

We all have so much to learn. There are so many unanswered questions. The space of what we do not know is infinite. But as Elder Jeffrey R. Holland has eloquently stated, "In this Church, what we know will always trump what we do not know."[21] The fuel in our tanks is always far more important and valuable than the empty space around it, regardless of how big that empty space is. This is true because the knowledge and testimony given to us by the Holy Ghost carries a weight that far exceeds secular knowledge or unanswered questions.

President Joseph Fielding Smith taught, "When a man has the manifestation from the Holy Ghost, it leaves an indelible impression on his soul, one that is not easily erased. It is Spirit speaking to spirit, and it comes with convincing force. A manifestation of an angel, or even of the Son of God himself, would impress the eye and mind, and eventually become dimmed, but the impressions of the Holy Ghost sink deeper into the soul and are more difficult to erase."[22]

I remember sitting in a Primary class as a young boy while visiting a family member's ward and watching a video of Joseph Smith's First Vision. The feeling of that moment is etched in my heart as the Spirit bore witness to me that God the Father and his Son, Jesus Christ, appeared to the boy Joseph. I remember one late night as a seminary-aged young man, lying in my bed reading the Book of Mormon. Suddenly, tears began to stream down my face as I received the overwhelming and unmistakable witness from the Holy Ghost that the people I was reading about were real and that the book was true.

I can reflect on countless moments as a missionary, sitting in someone's home teaching the restored gospel, when the Holy Ghost was present and there was so much peace, and we knew that what

---

21. Jeffrey R. Holland, "Lord, I Believe," *Ensign*, May 2013, 94.

22. Joseph Fielding Smith, *Answers to Gospel Questions*, comp. Joseph Fielding Smith Jr. (1966), 2:151.

was being taught was true and that our Heavenly Father wanted His children to know it.

I've sat in counsel with ward members struggling with addiction, abuse, marital problems, financial struggles, fear, anxiety, hopelessness, and sin. I've watched our Savior, Jesus Christ, perform countless miracles in their lives and make permanent, rescuing changes where no earthly influence could. I've been present when the Holy Ghost entered the room to give a confirming witness of the gospel to someone who was desperately and sincerely seeking it. I've felt God's love for His children when they couldn't feel it themselves.

I've had my own personal experiences when the Savior has changed me to become better, when I've repented of and been cleansed of sins, and when I knew those changes came because of the Atonement of Jesus Christ.

These personal, sacred experiences, along with countless others, are ingrained in my soul. They are impossible to ignore or forget, and I cannot deny them no matter what questions may arise in life. And when questions arise for me, I can reflect back on those sacred experiences as a foundation for my testimony.

You have very likely had similar experiences.

Elder Dieter F. Uchtdorf stated, "We *believe* in God because of things we *know* with our heart and mind, not because of things we *do not know*. Our spiritual experiences are sometimes too sacred to explain in worldly terms, but that doesn't mean they are not real."[23]

The witnesses of truth we have received from the Spirit, and the spiritual experiences we have had, can act like anchors to our faith when questions arise. If it was true when we received it, it's true now. So it's okay to follow Peter's example of faith by looking back to the Savior and relying on those past experiences when times get tough and a sea of doubt threatens our faith and testimony.

Questioning Spiritual Experiences

I am very much aware that one of the most common challenges members of the Church face when they pass through a trial of faith

---

23. Dieter F. Uchtdorf, "Be Not Afraid, Only Believe," *Ensign*, Nov. 2015, 78; emphasis in original.

is that they may question the witnesses of the Spirit and spiritual experiences they have received. This was the case with my friend Beth, whose story I shared previously. Beth had received multiple confirmations throughout her life regarding the Book of Mormon and the truthfulness of the restored gospel. But she arrived at a point in life when she started to wonder if those experiences were really from God or just in her own mind.

This is completely normal and understandable. "How do I know when I'm feeling the Spirit?" is always among the most frequent questions Church members ask. Learning to distinguish between our own thoughts and emotions and the impressions of the Holy Ghost is a skill that every member of the Church works to develop throughout their lives.

If you are having this experience of not being as sure as you once were about your past spiritual impressions and experiences, that's okay. We'll discuss later the topic of recognizing the voice of the Spirit and answers to our questions. But for now, consider a few simple suggestions that might be helpful.

First, it's okay to seek confirmation from heaven. Remember the brief story we just shared about Oliver Cowdery. The Lord had previously given Oliver spiritual confirmation about the divine authenticity of the work of the Restoration and the translation of the Book of Mormon. But Oliver obviously had subsequent experiences that caused him to wonder if those spiritual impressions were correct. And that's okay. Oliver sought a confirmation from the Lord, and the Lord was more than happy to give it. "I tell thee these things that thou mayest know that thou hast been enlightened by the Spirit of truth," the Lord told Oliver (Doctrine and Covenants 6:15).

The Lord loves us. He fully understands the set of experiences and actions in our lives that can give rise to doubt. He is more than willing to reconfirm the witness of truth we've already received if we sincerely seek it. And as it was for Oliver, and for my friend Beth, that reconfirmation can be a sweet experience and an opportunity to feel Heavenly Father's love. So if we believe we need a confirmation of our witness, we can add that to our list of questions to ponder and to humbly ask the Lord.

Second, the purpose of this book is to provide the tools to obtain the answers and clarity we are seeking. I believe that if we put forth the effort to do the things described here—by remembering God's mercy for ourselves and others, seeking revelation from heaven, converting doubts into sincere questions, remembering the witness of the Spirit and our past spiritual experiences, seeking help from priesthood leaders, studying, praying, repenting, and seeking to keep the commandments—then the clarity regarding the validity of our past spiritual experiences will come.

Act in Faith: Capture Your Spiritual Experiences

We've done the work of identifying our sincere questions to ponder and ask the Lord. If we use Brother Wilcox's analogy, we've identified the important empty space in the gas tank. I invite each of us now to do the same exercise the wonderful young women of my ward did those many years ago at camp.

Prayerfully consider and write down the following:

- Write down the things you know to be true because of the witness of the Holy Ghost. You might consider those things you know in your heart regarding your relationship with your Heavenly Father and your Savior, Jesus Christ; about the Restoration of the gospel; and about any other element of truth that the Holy Ghost has embedded in your heart.
- Write down the experiences in your life when you believe you felt the presence of the Holy Ghost or God's love for you.
- We'll add a third: For each of the above, how has this truth or experience changed you? How is your life different because of these experiences? What do each of these mean to you personally?

I again share my witness of the great importance of remembering and holding on to the light and knowledge we've already received through the Holy Ghost when our testimonies are challenged.

When Peter began to sink in the Sea of Galilee because of momentary fear and doubt, he knew enough to look back to the source of truth he could rely on. He looked back to the Savior and cried out,

"Lord, save me" (Matthew 14:30). That faith came because of Peter's past experiences with the Savior. Sometimes looking unto Christ in every thought means looking backward to the moments when we've felt closest to Him and holding on to those experiences while we press forward through stormy seas.

I hope that remembering your past spiritual experiences will, as it has for me, give you a sweet reminder of the great love our Heavenly Father has for you and His willingness to send the Holy Ghost to bear witness of truth when we sincerely ask in faith.

Principle 5: Seek Help from Priesthood Leaders

"And he gave some, apostles; and some, prophets; and some, evangelists; and some, pastors and teachers; For the perfecting of the saints, for the work of the ministry, for the edifying of the body of Christ: Till we all come in the unity of the faith, and of the knowledge of the Son of God." (Ephesians 4:11–13)

When Amy was struggling with her testimony of the gospel, she was hesitant to share her concerns with others. She worried that her doubts might affect her relationships with friends, family, or ward members. She feared that sharing her concerns might harm the faith and testimony of others. She did confide in her husband and a few very close friends, but she certainly did not want to tell her bishop what she was going through. She worried he might think less of her. She worried he would dismiss her doubts or try to refute them.

Amy tried several times to convince herself that she should simply suppress her concerns and just go on pretending to live the life of a content Church member for the sake of her family. But her doubts and the associated anxieties she experienced were gradually beginning to consume her life, exhausting her spiritually, mentally, and emotionally. The very underpinnings of her reality—the foundation upon which she'd made all her life decisions to this point, and the experiences that shaped her view of God and her own identity—were all being shaken, and she didn't know how to find her way through it.

Finally, the time came for Amy to renew her temple recommend. She didn't feel like she even wanted to attend the temple given her concerns, much less have an interview with her bishop where she knew she'd be asked questions about her testimony. But when the ward executive secretary called to schedule an appointment, she accepted. She thought about canceling, but at the encouragement of her loving husband, she went.

It's common for the Spirit to give promptings to bishops concerning the well-being of their ward members, and Amy's bishop could recognize beforehand that she was struggling. She sat in her bishop's office feeling anxious and uneasy. But instead of conducting a temple recommend interview, Amy's bishop began to sincerely ask how she was doing and how things were at home and with her husband and her children. Finally, he asked, "Amy, how are you feeling about your testimony?" With trepidation, she began to open up that she was having doubts about the Church because of some of the things she'd encountered on the internet.

Amy's bishop listened openly to her concerns without judging her. He did not try to convince her that her feelings were invalid. One thing Amy had been struggling with was feelings of guilt because of the doubts she was having. After all, she'd had many witnesses of the restored gospel. Having doubts felt like she was contradicting that knowledge. It made her feel unworthy.

"Amy," her bishop said, "you are keeping your covenants. You are living the gospel. You are trying to do the right things. You just have concerns that you need help resolving. And that's okay. The Lord loves you. He wants you to come to Him with your questions."

"You mean . . ." Amy said through genuine tears of relief, "that this doesn't mean I'm not worthy?"

"Of course not," her bishop responded.

Instead of renewing her temple recommend, Amy and her bishop determined that this was an opportunity for her to turn to Christ and seek answers to her questions. It would take months of sincere and faithful effort in study, prayer, and counseling with her bishop before Amy would feel ready to return to the temple. But the decision to share her concerns with her bishop was a pivotal, life-changing moment that began that process. Amy left that interview with a sense of relief and renewed hope. "This feels so right," she said as she left the bishop's office. "Thank you."

A Personal Witness of Priesthood Keys

Bishops and stake presidents are called, set apart, and given priesthood keys to serve as the presiding high priest and as "judges in Israel" for the members of their wards and stakes. In these sacred responsibilities, the Lord blesses bishops and stake presidents with spiritual gifts, talents, Christlike attributes, and revelation beyond their natural capabilities for the express purpose of helping each Church member, in their individual and unique moments of need, in their journey to come unto Christ.

I vividly remember visiting with our beloved bishop in his office a few days before I was to be set apart to take his place. I was scared to death of the calling that lay before me, and I didn't even fully understand what I was in for at that time. I had served as his counselor and we'd become good friends, but I knew I had only observed a small fraction of what he experienced as the bishop of our ward.

The bishop explained to me how to review financial reports, how to use the bishop's storehouse order forms, where he kept records and notes, how to provide financial assistance when needed, and a host of other administrative things. I was pretty sure that was the easy stuff that I could probably figure out on my own—it was not at all what I was anxious about.

"Do you have any questions?" he finally asked.

"Yes," I responded. "When someone comes into your office and needs help . . . how do you know what to say?!"

He paused for a few moments, looked at me with a slight but serious smile, and said, "You'll just know. It just comes."

That was it! I think he could tell I hoped for a more detailed answer. We talked a little more about being worthy and prepared spiritually and listening to the voice of the Spirit.

I have since experienced the great blessing and sacred responsibility of serving as a bishop in the Savior's church, The Church of Jesus Christ of Latter-day Saints. Through that experience, I became intensely aware of Christ's divine ability to utilize His ordained representatives to bless and rescue God's children. I'd like to share just a little of what that experience was like and how I believe it pertains to us in our search for truth.

While serving as bishop, my heart and mind were filled with promptings, thoughts, ideas, words, concerns, worries, empathy, and overwhelming love on behalf of the members of my ward. That revelation seemed nearly nonstop, perhaps with brief pauses only to allow me to focus on my own life and family. I came to know that Heavenly Father was personally and intimately involved in the details of the lives of each one of His children in my ward.

I would often feel prompted to study certain topics in great depth or to prepare and organize thoughts on a specific subject, only to find that the Lord was preparing me beforehand to provide needed counsel uniquely for one of my ward members. I would sometimes experience unexpected feelings or concerns for seemingly no apparent reason, and then I'd discover shortly thereafter that the Lord was allowing me to develop empathy through experience for the situation of a ward member who would need counsel.

Many times, when an individual would come into my office to speak with me, the Spirit would have already prepared me over the past several days, weeks, or months to receive them. Other times, a ward member would share something with me I was not anticipating, but the Spirit would provide the words, thoughts, ideas, and direction needed to help the individual move forward.

It sometimes seemed as though the Savior had a pre-planned schedule. As soon as one ward member's healing experience drew to an end, another's would shortly begin. The Lord seemed limited only by my capacity and time and the readiness and willingness of people to hear Him.

I spent countless hours with ward members striving to help each individual through their diverse and unique experiences—striving to help them repent of sins, overcome addictions, heal from the deep spiritual and emotional wounds of trauma or abuse, rescue marriages, overcome fear and doubt, receive a witness of the gospel, feel God's love for them, or simply make important life decisions. In these experiences, I was a firsthand witness and participant as I observed Christ work miracles in their lives—tearing down years of hurt and pain, transforming them, and helping them to really come to know and trust Him.

The blessing to participate so intimately in Christ's work to redeem His people changed me, and I will forever cherish the experience.

The Release

I have also had the experience of being released from that calling and having all that revelation on behalf of others end almost instantly. The contrast is so stark that many bishops describe it as a withdrawal of the Spirit. "It feels like you've done something wrong," one former bishop described to me, trying to prepare me for my release. "But you haven't."

I once asked a beloved former stake president how he was feeling a week after his release. "Up until a week ago," he replied, "my mind was a beehive of activity regarding the members of this stake. And then it all stopped when I was released."

On another occasion, this same good man told me, "You have gifts and talents as bishop that you will no longer have when you are released." He was right.

Elder Robert D. Hales, then serving as a newly called Presiding Bishop, reflected, "There is a hopeless feeling when you are released as a bishop to become a General Authority, and then return to your home ward where you have been serving and realize you have lost the power of discernment with the ward members. You can't do what you did as a bishop."[24]

It's no wonder many bishops and stake presidents feel a bit lost after being released. All the revelation they were accustomed to receiving on behalf of their ward and stake goes away and leaves a pretty vacant space behind.

Now, in sharing these thoughts, please note that by no means do I believe that I was a perfect bishop. I don't believe there is one. I made many mistakes in my service, and I know for a fact that many gracious ward members could attest to the things I should have done better. But I share these personal thoughts to bear witness that the

---

24. Robert D. Hales, "The Mantle of a Bishop," *Ensign*, May 1985, 28.

keys attendant with the calling of a priesthood leader are real and truly come from the Lord. In attendance with those callings, the Lord temporarily provides His representatives with spiritual gifts far beyond their natural capability for the singular purpose of blessing and helping *us* in our journey to come unto Christ. The Lord knows and loves each of us individually, and He has specifically called our leaders at this time to be able to help us.

The Adversary Tries to Separate Us from Priesthood Leaders

"Why didn't you come to see me sooner?" I found myself asking ward members that question time and time again after they'd finally worked up the courage to come talk to their bishop about struggles they needed help with. The responses varied. "I wanted to get past this on my own." "I worried about what you might think." "I just felt so ashamed." "I didn't think you could help." "I didn't want to burden you with this." These are just some of the reasons ward members would give for not taking that necessary and important step of seeking help from their priesthood leader.

If you have ever gone to seek help from your bishop or stake president, you understand full well the wrestle that takes place before you take that daunting step. Whatever the issue is, we first start to wonder, "Is this something I should talk to my bishop about?" Over a period of minutes, hours, days, weeks, or sometimes even months or years, the Holy Ghost prompts us repeatedly to "go see your bishop." And each time that prompting comes, the adversary moves in and starts to fill our mind with all kinds of rationalizations about why we should not or do not need to take that step.

When we are passing through any kind of a trial of faith, it is essential to understand that one of Satan's most common tactics—and one that he will absolutely, without question, employ on each of us—is to try to convince us that we should not or do not need to seek help from our priesthood leaders. I believe there are at least two reasons he uses this tactic.

First, Christ has called and chosen His servants and given them priesthood keys to represent Him so that He can reach us through them. Looking to our leaders for help means looking to Christ. And looking to Christ is the absolute last thing the adversary wants us to do in a trial of faith. The adversary will work to separate us from every source of divine help Christ has put in place for us.

Sister Sheri Dew shared these words from a wise stake president as he gave counsel to struggling members of his stake: "Please understand that Satan will do everything he can to encourage you to separate yourself from those who hold priesthood keys. My plea is that, regardless of the nature of your personal struggles, you don't ever succumb to that temptation. Those who hold keys can help you and guide you in ways others cannot."[25]

Second, Satan works in darkness. If he can convince us to keep something hidden, then he has exclusive access to work the problem on us. It's like being locked in a spiritual boxing ring—just us and the adversary. And given his age, wisdom, and unveiled memory, he has the advantage over us. He will attempt to keep us there until he has won the battle over our heart and mind. But when we bring a problem out into the light, Satan loses his hold and the problem can now be worked out with help from the Savior's representatives and the Holy Ghost.

An Act of Faith in Christ

For those struggling with doubts about their testimony of the restored gospel, let me identify what I think are the most common concerns that might be keeping us from reaching out to our bishop or stake president for help.

- We may believe that our priesthood leader is unable to help for lack of experience, understanding, or knowledge.
- We may believe that our priesthood leader has chosen to live on blind faith and is therefore either unaware of or unwilling to acknowledge the issues, information, and feelings that are causing us to have doubts about the Church.

25. Sheri L. Dew, *Worth the Wrestle* (Salt Lake City, UT: Deseret Book, 2017), Deseret Bookshelf.

- Our doubts about the gospel may be leading us to a general mistrust of all Church leaders, including our bishop or stake president.
- We may be worried about the consequences of confessing or sharing that we are having doubts about the restored gospel. We may worry that our priesthood leader will judge us or think less of us for expressing our concerns. We may even have a friendship with our leaders that we worry will be tainted.
- In the process of having doubts about the restored gospel, we may have made choices that have led us away from the covenant path. We may have committed serious or minor transgressions that now seem overwhelmingly daunting to confront. And we may now be worried about the difficult task or consequences of working through the repentance process with our bishop or stake president.
- We may have had past experiences with priesthood leaders where we've have felt offended and find it difficult to consider seeking their guidance.

I am not going to suggest that these concerns are invalid. Bishops, stake presidents, and elders quorum, Relief Society, and Young Women presidents are all imperfect people, and each one is unique in their knowledge, experiences, wisdom, and character. As mentioned, I'm personally aware of many mistakes I made while serving as bishop, and I'm sure my ward members are aware of even more. I inadvertently offended some members. And there were times when I wished I'd had better counsel to offer.

But if any of the concerns we've listed are dissuading us from acting on promptings from the Holy Ghost to reach out to our priesthood leaders for help, perhaps a few considerations will help.

First, the decision to involve our priesthood leader in our struggles with our testimony of the gospel is not an act of faith in our priesthood leader; it is an act of faith in Christ and in His ability to bless us through them despite their limitations and imperfections. When we walk into that office, we are signaling to the Savior our faith in Him and our desire to do the right thing. If the Holy Ghost is prompting us to act, we can take confidence that such a step will lead us down the right path. The Lord will bless us for taking action in faith.

Second, as we've already discussed, the Savior imparts gifts, talents, and abilities to His priesthood leaders to help us according to *our* faith. They become the instrument, and the Lord can grant them custom-tailored revelation for us beyond their capability because of *our* faith in Christ. We have reason to hope and believe that Christ will work through our priesthood leaders to uniquely help us. Through my own experience, I can say that there's a good chance the Lord has already been preparing your bishop or stake president with feelings and insights to know how to help you.

Finally, Christ has a loving, kind, patient, forgiving disposition. It is His nature. It is my experience that He imparts that disposition upon His representatives. They begin to feel and think about us the way the Savior does.

Elder Robert D. Hales, also while serving as Presiding Bishop, taught, "All members of the Church can turn to their bishops when they are in need of help and can feel secure in his love for them and can have confidence in following his counsel. Bishops learn not to judge people against a standard of perfection. A bishop learns that he will rejoice with those over whom he presides in any progress they make."[26]

Knowing the great struggle we go through to finally take those heavy steps into the bishop's office, my first response to those brave ward members would always be something like this: "Thank you for coming. I know how hard it is to work up the courage to do this. You were right to come talk to me. You've followed the promptings of the Holy Ghost to be here. The Lord loves you, and all He wants to do is help you. And I'm here to help with that." We'd turn to the words of the Savior in the scriptures to find hope, then we'd seek the guidance of the Holy Ghost to figure out how to get to work so they could move forward.

Please don't ever be afraid to talk to your bishop or stake president. They love you and the Lord loves you. Nothing you can do or

---

26. Robert D. Hales, "The Mantle of a Bishop," *Ensign*, May 1985, 29.

say will change that. They want nothing more than to help you, and the Lord can work through them to bless you.

Act in Faith: Reach Out for Help

How do we know if we should talk to our priesthood leader? If the thought has come to our mind, more than once, that we should visit with our bishop or stake president, even if we've dismissed it, we can be almost certain that it's a prompting from the Holy Ghost and that we should follow it. The Spirit will keep giving us that prompting until we either acknowledge and act on it or we can no longer hear His voice (see Ether 2:15; 1 Nephi 17:45).

So the invitation to act in this principle is to "yield to the enticings of the Holy Spirit" (Mosiah 3:19), put off our natural fears, and take that step. Make the decision to seek the help of your priesthood leader as you work through this trial of your faith. Call or message the executive secretary and schedule an appointment. Then pray for courage and ask the Lord to bless your priesthood leader with the inspiration they need specifically for you. Along with any anxiety we may feel, we will feel the Holy Ghost encouraging us along, and we'll also feel a sense of hope. That encouragement from the Spirit is a confirming witness that we're doing the right thing.

I wanted to share one final important note before we conclude this principle. While I have largely spoken from my personal experience having served as a bishop, Young Women presidents and Relief Society presidents are also called, set apart, and given authority under the direction of priesthood keys to receive revelation for members of their organizations. Elders quorum presidents also hold priesthood keys to receive revelation on behalf of the members of their quorum. These leaders can be very powerful allies in our struggle to regain or develop our witness of the restored gospel, and the Spirit may prompt us to reach out to one of these leaders as our primary line of help. The Lord will bless us through these leaders as we act on those promptings.

While I don't know what your specific experience will be like as you seek help from your leaders, I hope you'll feel similar to this sister who expressed these words of gratitude to her bishop after finally seeking help through her trial of faith: "This process is foreign to me—working with a bishop. It is new and different but so good. I feel like

I have never had anyone care about me and want to help me so much. Thank you for that."

Whatever our experience is, I know that as we demonstrate our faith in Christ by seeking help from priesthood leaders, we will feel the encouragement of the Holy Ghost and the Lord will direct and guide us to the next steps in our journey. I will ever be in awe of how far Christ will go—or how far He will send one of His servants—to rescue one of God's children.

Exercises

Ponder the following questions and write down your thoughts.

- Consider the verses found in Ephesians 4:11–14. What do you learn about why the Lord gives us Church leaders?
- Consider the Savior's experience in Mark 6:1–6 when He visited His hometown. What prevented Christ from performing miracles for the people there? Contrast this with the Savior's experience among the Nephites as recorded in 3 Nephi 19:35–36. How might our faith affect Christ's ability to bless us through priesthood leaders?

Principle 6: Seek Learning by Study

"Search the scriptures—search the revelations . . . and ask your Heavenly Father, in the name of His Son Jesus Christ, to manifest the truth unto you, and if you do it with an eye single to His glory nothing doubting, He will answer you by the power of His Holy Spirit. You will then know for yourselves and not for another. You will not then be dependent on man for the knowledge of God; nor will there be any room for speculation." (Joseph Smith)[27]

We've now done the work to identify our most important sincere questions. We've taken time to ponder and remember the past spiritual experiences and witnesses of truth we've already been given. Hopefully we've also turned to our priesthood leaders for inspired help and guidance. We now turn our attention to searching for answers to our questions through study.

Recall that the first principle we shared is that answers to the questions that matter most can only come by revelation from heaven through the divine witness of the Holy Ghost. Intellectual pursuits and human reason alone cannot replace that confirming spiritual witness. However, the Lord has also instructed us to "seek learning, even by study, and also by faith" (Doctrine and Covenants 88:118).

27. *Teachings of the Prophet Joseph Smith*, sel. Joseph Fielding Smith (1976), 11–12.

The Oxford Dictionary defines *study* as "the devotion of time and attention to acquiring knowledge."[28] Devoting time and attention to acquiring a knowledge of the truths of the gospel is a form of work. Gospel study is a form of acting in faith. Sincere study is part of the work we do to create the environment within us to receive revelation and a witness of truth through the Holy Ghost. We look to Christ and act in faith when we seek answers from heaven through intelligent, spiritually directed study.

In these next few chapters, we discuss the principles that govern effective gospel study in search of answers to our sincere questions. We'll start by studying the process by which we grow in knowledge of truth. Understanding this process will enable us to determine where to prioritize our time and attention as we seek learning through the Holy Ghost "by study, and also by faith" (Doctrine and Covenants 88:118).

The Truth Shall Make You Free

How important is it to develop a knowledge of what is true and what is false? The Savior and His prophets have taught that a knowledge of truth is essential to our happiness and freedom. When Jesus addressed an unbelieving group of Pharisees, he told them they were in bondage, or captivity, because they could not recognize, accept, and act on the truth of His words "because [His] word [had] no place in [them]" (John 8:37).

Conversely, to those in the same crowd who believed His words, the Savior indicated that their ability to recognize and accept truth would free them from captivity. "If ye continue in my word," He stated, "then are ye my disciples indeed; And ye shall know the truth, and the truth shall make you free" (John 8:31–32).

President Dieter F. Uchtdorf elaborated on this relationship between knowledge and freedom, saying, "It is knowledge of truth that makes us free to exercise our moral agency and freedom of choice."[29]

---

28. *Oxford English Dictionary*, s.v. "study," accessed October 24, 2023, https://www.oed.com/dictionary/study_n.

29. Dieter F. Uchtdorf, "Truth Restored" (Brigham Young University devotional, Aug. 22, 2006), 2, speeches.byu.edu.

Likewise, the Prophet Joseph Smith taught, "A man is saved no faster than he gets knowledge, for if he does not get knowledge, he will be brought into captivity."[30]

In other words, without a correct knowledge of truth, we ultimately do not know what to do, how to live, or how to act in accordance with true principles that lead to eternal life and happiness. Without that knowledge, we are held captive, incapable of moving forward.

In reality, we live this principle every day. In all our daily pursuits for earthly knowledge—in our many internet searches and our time spent in school—our purpose is the same. Whether the topic is parenting, do-it-yourself projects, home decorating, health care, or anything else, we are trying to obtain knowledge on some subject in order to know how to act to solve a problem and thus move forward and make progress. Without that knowledge, we remain stuck.

This is why it's so essential to have a knowledge of our divine nature, our relationship to our Heavenly Father, the reality of Jesus Christ's Atonement, and the Restoration of the gospel. Our search for answers to our sincere questions has far more implications than just developing a testimony. Our eternal progress and happiness hang in the balance.

The Process of Growing in Light and Truth

The process of recognizing, acquiring, and acting on pure knowledge is fundamental to our identity as sons and daughters of God. The Lord revealed that intelligence and truth are part of who we are and who we are meant to become. Truth is part of our spiritual makeup. "Man was also in the beginning with God," the Savior taught. "Intelligence, or the light of truth, was not created or made, neither indeed can be" (Doctrine and Covenants 93:29).

The Savior also explained that intelligence, light, and truth are part of the exaltation and glory that our Heavenly Father has attained: "The glory of God is intelligence, or, in other words, light and truth" (Doctrine and Covenants 93:36).

Our ultimate potential as sons and daughters of God is obtained as we increase in light and truth until we also are made perfect like our

30. Joseph Smith, in *History of the Church*, 4:588.

heavenly parents. The Lord described this process of growing in truth when He taught, "That which is of God is light; and he that receiveth light, and continueth in God, receiveth more light; and that light groweth brighter and brighter until the perfect day" (Doctrine and Covenants 50:24). And also, "He that keepeth [the] commandments receiveth truth and light, until he is glorified in truth and knoweth all things" (Doctrine and Covenants 93:28).

The process of growing in a knowledge of the truth described in these verses is fairly simple. Broken into steps, it looks something like this:

- God makes truth available to us.
- As we recognize, accept, and act on truth, we gradually grow in glory and intelligence until we eventually possess a fulness of truth like our Heavenly Father.
- Living a fulness of truth brings a fulness of joy.

Seems pretty straightforward, right? However, our own life experience tells us it's not quite that easy. And this is where it gets difficult for us as we seek answers to our questions through study. A few essential elements come into the picture that complicate this process of attaining and living a knowledge of truth. They are agency and opposition.

Agency to Accept Truth

Our Heavenly Father never forces us to accept or live truth. He does everything He can to make truth available to us, but He allows us to exercise our agency to decide what level of intelligence we are comfortable attaining and living. He does, however, warn us of the consequences of rejecting truth. As it states in Doctrine and Covenants 93:31–32, "Behold, here is the agency of man, and here is the condemnation of man; because that which was from the beginning is plainly manifest unto them, and they receive not the light. And every man whose spirit receiveth not the light is under condemnation,"

Condemnation? That seems pretty strong, doesn't it? What does the Lord mean when He says we're under condemnation when we don't receive truth?

Simply put, when truth is made available to us and we choose to reject it, we limit our own opportunity to increase in knowledge and capability. Our progress is stalled or reversed. In other words, we "condemn" ourselves, or lead ourselves away from salvation and into captivity, when we exercise our agency to reject an increase in intelligence.

So, with our agency—our freedom to choose—also comes the freedom to limit ourselves when we willingly reject light and truth. When we wrestle with our agency, we are often conflicted in our desires to find truth. We may wrestle with underlying desires to act contrary to the commandments of God, the counsel of living prophets and apostles, or the everyday demands of living the gospel. Or we may feel caught between living the gospel and feeling in harmony with our family members, friends, or community regarding challenging social issues.

The Natural Man

There is another element worth identifying as a challenge to finding truth as it relates to our agency. That is our own "natural man." As we learn from King Benjamin in the Book of Mormon, "The natural man is an enemy to God, and has been from the fall of Adam" (Mosiah 3:19).

The desires and appetites of our own natural, mortal tabernacles can blind us to truth. Sometimes the desire to satisfy those mortal appetites of pride, fear, lust, or physical stimulus can lead us to reject truth in order to rationalize or justify our actions.

A dear friend of mine, after returning to the restored gospel after many years of inactivity, shared with me that he'd left the Church as a young adult because he felt the rules were oppressive and he really wanted to indulge in immorality, drugs, and partying. In retrospect, he realized he had used controversial topics in Church history to justify a belief that the restored gospel was false so that he could feel comfortable with the life he wanted to live at that time. Now, many years later, the Lord had found ways to bring him back to the Church, and he better understood the experience he was going through in his younger years.

We would be wise to recognize that our own natural desire to act contrary to truth or wise counsel from God can be a powerful deterrent to hearing the voice of the Spirit and accepting truth.

Opposition in Our Search for Truth

Where many sincere members of the Church get stuck may not be related to their desire to find truth. After all, most of us want to know and do the right thing. Where many sincere Church members struggle, as my dear friend Amy did, is with the opposition and confusion that arise when they try to find truth.

The Lord warns us of several elements of opposition we can expect to encounter as we exercise our agency to pursue a knowledge of truth. It is essential to know that we will absolutely encounter this opposition as we embark on a search for answers to our questions through study.

The Lord stated, "And that wicked one cometh and taketh away light and truth, through disobedience, from the children of men, and because of the tradition of their fathers" (Doctrine and Covenants 93:39).

The Adversary

The first element the Lord identified that seeks to lead us away from truth is "that wicked one" (Doctrine and Covenants 93:39), or Satan.

It should be no surprise that Satan is bent on keeping us away from truth. He is an enemy to all truth, having exercised his own agency to reject and distance himself from truth. Christ described Satan's nature in relation to truth when He explained, "He [Satan] was a murderer from the beginning, and abode not in the truth, because there is no truth in him . . . for he is a liar, and the father of it" (John 8:44).

Satan is motivated. He is miserable and would like our company (see 2 Nephi 2:27). He is bent on leading away as many of God's children as possible, still hoping to prove that Heavenly Father's plan of agency is a failure and to obtain power over as many others as possible (see Moses 4:1–3). Satan seeks to bring us into captivity through ignorance.

Because Satan knows we have a desire to know and live the truth, his best approach is not to try to convince us to accept blatant falsehood but instead to attempt to make the truth indistinguishable. For example, I'm convinced Satan was the mastermind behind putting "fat-free" on candy labels to convince me that my favorite licorice is great for weight loss. If Satan can confuse us about what is true, he can keep us in captivity, unable to act in truth and righteousness.

Satan will attempt to blur the line between truth and error just long enough to lead us to exercise our agency to move away from the gospel and eventually into sin, transgression, and captivity. His goal is to get us to make choices that diminish the light and truth within us until we either cannot find our way back to Christ or no longer desire to.

"And thus he whispereth in their ears," Nephi taught, "until he grasps them with his awful chains, from whence there is no deliverance" (2 Nephi 28:21).

The Traditions of Men

The second element of opposition the Lord identified that leads us away from truth is "the traditions of [our] fathers" (Doctrine and Covenants 93:39). I believe this statement refers to any man-made societal or cultural traditions, philosophies, ideas, policies, or behaviors that are not founded in truth and thus either intentionally or unintentionally lead to misinformation and confusion.

In other words, Satan does not get all the credit. We have demonstrated that we are quite capable of generating and promoting our own false ideas. And our technologically advanced information age has made all of those false ideas instantly accessible.

One of the primary struggles many Church members encounter when they have questions about the restored gospel is sifting through the massive amount of information and commentary available to identify valid sources of truth.

Brother Matthew Grow, Church Historian, stated, "We all know that the challenge in the information age is not to find answers—we're surrounded by answers—but to discern between good answers and bad answers, good information and bad information."[31]

So heads up—the Lord has given us advanced warning that when we embark on a sincere search for answers to our questions and a witness of the restored gospel, we can be absolutely certain that we are going to run into a barrage of hundreds and thousands of years' worth of foolish traditions, false ideas, and fake wisdom of the world. That warning should be enough to make us aware that we can't go through this process haphazardly. We've got to be wise and deliberate, armed with an understanding of how God guides us to truth.

Reflection: Agency or Opposition?

Having discussed agency and opposition in our search for truth, it's worth taking a moment here for personal reflection. When we are struggling with our witness of the restored gospel, it may be worth pausing to ask ourselves, "Am I struggling with opposition in finding the truth? Or am I struggling with my own agency? Am I searching for truth? Or am I looking to rationalize not living the gospel so that I can live the life I think I want to live?" Being honest with ourselves is empowering as we move forward.

In reality, we each experience opposition and conflicting desires in our search for truth. The good news is the Lord knows how to help us with both. As we act in faith according to true principles and give the Holy Ghost opportunity to speak to our hearts and minds, the Lord can develop within us the desire and strength to exercise our agency to seek and embrace pure knowledge while He also guides us to truth.

The Spirit Testifies of Truth

So what are we to do now that we've added opposition and agency to this experience of acquiring truth? Are we abandoned to distinguish truth from error based solely on our individual intellectual ability? That would truly be a bleak prospect, wouldn't it? None of us has enough time, energy, wisdom, or access to information to succeed

---

31. Matthew J. Grow, "Worldwide Devotional for Young Adults: A Face to Face Event with Elder Quentin L. Cook" (worldwide young adult broadcast, Sept. 9, 2018), broadcasts.ChurchofJesusChrist.org.

at such an endeavor. Fortunately, Heavenly Father has never required that from His children.

As we discussed in our first principle, our Heavenly Father has never left His children alone in their search for truth. From the beginning of time, long before the internet existed as a source of information, and even before books were written, the Lord has given us the Holy Ghost to "teach [us] all things, . . . bring all things unto [our] remembrance" (John 14:26), and help us "know the truth of all things" (Moroni 10:5).

The Savior explained the Spirit's role in guiding us home when He revealed, "And the Spirit giveth light to every man that cometh into the world; and the Spirit enlighteneth every man through the world, that hearkeneth to the voice of the Spirit. And every one that hearkeneth to the voice of the Spirit cometh unto God, even the Father" (Doctrine and Covenants 84:46–47).

We are not alone in our search for truth. We each have available to us a member of the Godhead whose mission and desire is to take us by the hand, cut through the falsehood and confusion created by Satan and the foolishness of men, and lead us safely on the path home to our Heavenly Father.

That gift is available to us regardless of our age, ethnicity, gender, economic status, access to earthly information, education, or intellectual background. We need only learn how to seek and recognize His voice.

Summary: The Process of Growing in Light and Truth

Let's summarize the process of growing in light and truth, taking into account the elements of agency, opposition, and the witness of the Holy Ghost.

- God makes truth available to us.
- The adversary, the voices of the world, and our own "natural man" create misinformation and confusion and make it difficult to discern truth from error.
- The Holy Ghost bears witness of truth and warns of error.

- We exercise our agency to accept or reject truth and the witness of the Spirit.
- As we recognize, accept, and act on truth, we gradually grow in glory and intelligence until we eventually possess a fulness of truth like our Heavenly Father. Living a fulness of truth brings a fulness of joy.
- As we reject truth, our progress is halted or reversed. We are held captive by a lack of knowledge and do not know how to act in righteousness.

We each experience this process as we search for truth through sincere study. In the next chapter, we will use our understanding of this process to identify those sources of information that have the highest likelihood of exposing us to truth and guiding us to answers to our questions through the witness of the Holy Ghost.

Act in Faith: Identifying Opposition in Your Life

Let's take action on what we've just learned about the process of growing in light and truth. Use your list of doubts and questions. For each question, consider the following:

- What sources of opposition or confusion have you been encountering in regard to finding truth as it relates to this question? These may be voices of opposition in the world or conflicting or confusing information.
- Are you experiencing conflicting desires in your search for truth regarding this question? What natural desires or social pressures may be making it difficult for you to receive truth on this topic?
- What promptings from the Holy Ghost has the Lord been trying to send you to bear witness of truth regarding this question?

Exercises

Ponder the following questions and write down your thoughts.

- What experiences have you had in your own life when you were able to progress by acquiring a knowledge of truth you previously did not have? These may be spiritual, temporal, educational, or intellectual experiences. Describe your experience and the effort you put forth in obtaining that knowledge. How did opposition and agency influence those experiences?
- In what ways might you or a loved one be held captive today (unable to progress) due to a lack of knowledge?
- Review the set of sincere questions you have written down. Do you feel to adjust any of your questions to better reflect the desires of your heart and the knowledge you are seeking? Do you feel you are starting to receive answers to any of your questions?

Seek Ye Out the Best Sources

"I know Heavenly Father loves and cares for me and has literally saved me in so many ways. I had a hard time going to sleep last night because the Spirit was so strong and I had a new feeling I haven't had before and a sense of peace and liberation I've been seeking for so long."

Amy recorded those words one morning after a particularly meaningful evening of immersed personal gospel study. When Amy had first visited with her bishop, her mind was wrapped up in concerning information she'd encountered about Church history and early Church leaders. She had been devoting her time and attention to finding knowledge primarily through studying commentary and opinions that she could most easily find on the internet, seeking to prove or disprove the doubts she'd begun to have about the restored gospel. These sources were not bringing her peace nor answering her questions.

We live in a time when access to information is readily available. Most of the answers to our daily, trivial questions can be answered instantly through a Google search. Our modern lives have conditioned us to believe that all our answers are available through a tap or click. We're accustomed to seeking answers to earthly questions through the wisdom, experience, and commentary of the internet masses. For example, I know that any time I need to repair the car, do some home improvement, compare the quality of products, decide which restaurant to visit or which movie to see, I rely heavily on the wisdom and experience of others on the internet. And that truly is a great blessing.

Given that reality, we may be tempted to believe that a witness of the restored gospel is obtainable through similar means. But answers to our most important spiritual questions are not obtained through this type of study. The process of growing in knowledge of truth is a divine process that is meant not merely to inform us but to transform us into new creatures, filled with light and truth. Information and opinion alone are insufficient. The truth must be "burned" into our souls and become a part of us.

The Lord has intentionally designed this life experience such that we must go to *Him* in our search for truth so that He can not only teach us but also change us. He needs us to "look unto [Him] in every thought" (Doctrine and Covenants 6:36) for answers. There is no shortcut or bypass route that gives us the knowledge we seek without going to Christ. Thus, the answers to our sincere gospel-related questions require not an internet connection but a heavenly connection. And as we learned in the first principle, the Holy Ghost is that connection.

It was not until Amy changed her approach to finding answers and began to look unto Christ in her sincere study efforts that she began to more clearly hear the voice of the Spirit. Through the Holy Ghost, she received the revelation and spiritual experiences that led to the feelings of divine love, peace, and liberation that she recorded that morning. Just as Amy experienced, sincere gospel study of the right sources can open the door to revelation and the closeness we seek with our Heavenly Father and Savior.

Principles to Guide Our Study

In the previous chapter, we studied the process of acquiring knowledge and growing in light and truth, including the opposition we encounter in that process. That process requires that we be exposed to truth, that the Holy Ghost bear witness of the truth, and that we exercise our agency to accept and live it.

Understanding that process, we can identify a few principles to use for determining ideal sources of information to study as we seek to resolve doubt and find answers to our sincere questions. Here are the principles we'll use:

- The primary purpose of our study is to provide opportunities for the Holy Ghost to bear witness of truth to our heart and mind.
- We significantly increase our opportunities to receive revelation and spiritual experiences when we intentionally increase our exposure to potential sources of divine truth.
- To reduce noise and confusion, we primarily allow sources to speak for themselves, and we allow the Holy Ghost to bear witness as to their truthfulness as opposed to seeking or relying on the opinion of others.

These principles support the process by which we obtain knowledge of light and truth. Now, you may be thinking we're being too narrow with these principles. Where do opinion, commentary, critical sources, or historical or scientific data fit into the picture? They do have a place, and we'll talk about those in the next chapter. But for now, we're just trying to establish principles for selecting sources that provide the highest opportunity for us to be exposed to and receive a witness of truth through the Holy Ghost. We're trying to turn down the noise for a moment, cut through the clutter, and get right to the point with the Spirit as our guide.

Primary Sources

Using our proposed principles, we can create a prioritized list of sources that maximize opportunity for the Holy Ghost to bear witness to our hearts of their truthfulness. Here, again, we look unto Christ for the example of how to select those ideal sources. The Savior cited these sources when He tried to help others know where to look for a witness of His divinity:

- The words of Christ and His servants as recorded in ancient and modern scripture (see John 5:39)
- The words of modern-day prophets, apostles, and other Church leaders (see John 5:32–33)

- Firsthand accounts, experiences, teachings, and documents (see John 8:14, 18)

When we are wrestling with doubt, confusion, and questions, we prioritize time with these primary sources because they cut out the middle-man commentary and opinion of others, giving the Holy Ghost unencumbered opportunity to bear direct witness of truth. These sources also provide opportunity for us to have the personal spiritual experiences we need. Let's briefly discuss each of these.

The Scriptures

The Apostle Paul wrote, "All scripture is given by inspiration of God, and is profitable for doctrine, for reproof, for correction, for instruction in righteousness: That the man of God may be perfect, throughly furnished unto all good works" (2 Timothy 3:16–17).

There is perhaps no more readily available and more instantly accessible source of divine inspiration and truth than the scriptures. The words of Christ and His servants are available at our fingertips anytime we want them. It is also humbling to me to think of the great care and sacrifice that has gone into the preservation of the words we have in the Bible, the Book of Mormon, and even the Doctrine and Covenants. Many individuals, inspired by the Lord, have sacrificed their lives and livelihoods to make the word of God accessible to us today. We are the beneficiaries of all their sacrifices.

If we're looking for answers to gospel questions, surely the scriptures ought to be one of our highest priority sources. There we can not only find answers to doctrinal questions, but we can feel the love of our Heavenly Father for us as we spend time with the Holy Ghost.

In a devotional given at BYU–Idaho, the late Clayton Christensen shared his personal experience of gaining a witness of the Book of Mormon. Elder Christensen recounted a moment in his life when, faced with the demands of a heavy graduate school curriculum and time-consuming church callings, he desperately needed to know if the Book of Mormon and the Church were true. He'd already read the Book of Mormon seven times in his life and never received that witness. He promised the Lord that if he could receive that witness, he would dedicate his life to building the Lord's kingdom on the earth, and that if it wasn't true, he would dedicate his life to finding out what was true.

Elder Christensen committed one hour every night to reading the Book of Mormon in his Oxford dorm room and praying to ask the Lord if it was true. He did this night after night. Elder Christensen later recounted how that witness of truth finally came to him:

> By the time I got to the chapters at the end of second Nephi, one evening when I said my prayer and sat in my chair and opened the book, all of a sudden there came into that room a beautiful, warm, loving spirit that just surrounded me and permeated my soul, and enveloped me in a feeling of love that I just had not imagined I could feel. And I began to cry, and I didn't want to stop crying because as I looked through my tears at the words in the Book of Mormon, I could see truth in those words that I never imagined I could comprehend before. And I could see the glories of eternity and I could see what God had in store for me as one of His sons. And I didn't want to stop crying. That spirit stayed with me the whole hour, and then every evening as I prayed and sat with the Book of Mormon by the fireplace in my room, that same spirit returned and it changed my heart and my life forever.[32]

Our experiences with the Spirit may be more gradual or subtle than Elder Christensen's. But that is the life-changing effect the scriptures can have on us. The words of Christ and His servants can bring not only a knowledge of truth but a life-changing personal relationship with God. That relationship can replace a whole host of doubts with firsthand personal knowledge and experience.

If we're seeking a witness that Jesus is the Christ, that the Book of Mormon is true, and that Joseph Smith was a prophet of God, certainly one of the fastest ways to cut through the noisy chatter of opinion in the world regarding those questions is to simply pick up the Bible, the Book of Mormon, and the Doctrine and Covenants and to prayerfully study, asking the Lord for a witness of their truthfulness. The scriptures are life-changing, high-quality source material in our search for truth.

---

32. Clayton M. Christensen, "Decisions for Which I've Been Grateful" (Brigham Young University–Idaho devotional, June 8, 2004), byui.edu.

The Words of Modern-Day Prophets, Apostles, and Church Leaders

Through the Prophet Joseph Smith, the Savior said regarding His servants, "And whatsoever they shall speak when moved upon by the Holy Ghost shall be scripture, shall be the will of the Lord, shall be the mind of the Lord, shall be the word of the Lord, shall be the voice of the Lord, and the power of God unto salvation" (Doctrine and Covenants 68:4).

When we are struggling with our testimony of the gospel because of confusion over complex or controversial topics, one of the best things we can do is to listen to or read what modern-day Church leaders have taught on these subjects. If we are sincerely seeking truth, the Holy Ghost can use their words to answer our sincere questions. He can also confirm to us whether their words are true. All the opinion and commentary in the world becomes secondary when we hear truth from the Lord through His servants and the Holy Ghost confirms it to our souls.

The words of Church leaders, like the scriptures, are almost instantly accessible in our internet age. At a few taps of a finger, we can listen to any general conference talk going back to 1971! Devotionals given by prophets, apostles, and other Church leaders at BYU, BYU–Idaho, and Ensign College are an trove of truth and are readily available online.

I used to spend my daily commute and workout times listening to the news or my favorite music station. Years ago, I made the decision to instead spend that time listening to the words of modern-day prophets, apostles, and other Church leaders. That decision completely changed my life. My car and the gym became sacred places where the Spirit could teach me, comfort me, open my mind to truth, and strengthen and fortify my testimony.

I cannot count the number of times I've gone to the Lord in desperate prayer—seeking answers to questions, or seeking guidance as a father or in my calling, or just needing comfort—and have had the Lord answer that prayer through the words of His servants that very hour or day. I still read the news, but that earthly insight pales in significance when compared to the knowledge and experiences I receive when I seek truth through the Lord's servants.

Firsthand Sources

This world is full of opinions about Jesus Christ, His restored Church, and His prophets and apostles. Some of these opinions are truthful and uplifting, but some are designed to mislead and cause confusion.

On multiple occasions, when the Savior was faced with false accusations about who He was and what He was teaching, He taught us which voices matter most in our search for truth. He explained, "It is also written in your law, that the testimony of two men is true. I am one that bear witness of myself, and the Father that sent me beareth witness of me" (John 8:17–18).

Have you ever been misunderstood or misrepresented, perhaps even intentionally? We would feel it quite unjust if everyone looked to the unfavorable opinion of others to seek the truth about our character and experiences when questions arise. We would hope to be given the opportunity to speak for ourselves. We can and should give that same opportunity when confronting our doubts by letting the original sources speak first and allowing the Holy Ghost to teach us.

What does going to original sources look like? Here are a few examples:

- When a question arises regarding the integrity and character of past Church leaders, we look to their personal accounts, teachings, and writings first and those with the closest personal relationships to them.
- When seeking a witness of the divinity of Jesus Christ, we look to His personal words and those of firsthand witnesses.
- When doubts arise over Church policies or doctrine, we first give sincere opportunity to Church leaders to help us understand the motivations and circumstances around such policies rather than going to the commentary, speculation, or criticism of others.

- When seeking a witness of the Book of Mormon, we study the Book of Mormon and let it speak first for itself.
- When seeking a witness of the Restoration of the gospel, we look first to the original sources: the Book of Mormon, the testimony of the Prophet Joseph Smith, the revelations contained in the Doctrine and Covenants, and the witnesses of the Book of Mormon and the Restoration.

I've often wondered how the Lord feels about the fact that He's gone out of His way to give us His words through the scriptures and prophets, and yet so often we cast all that aside and instead wholeheartedly look to the secondhand commentary and opinions of others.

When we are seeking truth regarding policies, doctrines, gospel topics, or historical events, surely one of the first and most fair things we should do is allow the original sources to speak first. The Holy Ghost can bear witness to the validity of those original sources, and He can do so without the noise of any earthly commentary.

The scriptures, the words of living prophets and Church leaders, and firsthand accounts are primary sources to study, providing maximum opportunity for the Lord to answer our sincere questions through revelation from heaven.

Act in Faith: Identify Your Primary Sources

We've established criteria for identifying ideal sources. And we've identified three categories of primary sources most likely to maximize opportunity to receive answers to our questions through revelation. One way we can act in faith is considering specific primary study sources for our questions.

Using the list of questions you have developed, consider the following:

- Scriptures: What scriptures could you study that would give the Holy Ghost opportunity to teach you regarding your question or doubt?
- The words of modern prophets, apostles, and other Church leaders: What talks or books have modern-day Church leaders given that touch on the subjects you have questions about? Is

there material that faithful friends and Church leaders have been inspired to suggest to you? You might counsel with your bishop, Relief Society president, elders quorum president, or Young Women president to see what talks or articles they might suggest.

- Firsthand sources: If you're struggling with doubts regarding the character of Church leaders, or historical events in Church history, or with certain Church policies or procedures, what firsthand sources can you study that would provide opportunity for the Holy Ghost to speak to your mind and heart regarding those subjects? Journals, letters, books, articles, Church news broadcasts, and talks from general conference are possible examples. The Joseph Smith Papers project, available online, contains thousands of writings of individuals with firsthand experiences in the Restoration of the Church. These writings give deep insight into their character and struggles. Statements issued by Church leaders regarding controversial subjects or Church policies provide a direct opportunity for the Spirit to give answers to our questions.

In this chapter, we've used the pattern by which we grow in light and truth to establish criteria for identifying sources of information that are most likely to increase our opportunity to receive revelation through the Holy Ghost. We've looked unto the Savior as our example to identify three types of sources that meet that criteria. And finally, we've acted in faith to do the work of identifying specific sources to study as we seek answers to our sincere questions.

It is my experience that as we deliberately provide opportunity for the Holy Ghost to bear witness of truth—through the words of scripture, modern prophets and leaders, and the firsthand accounts of others—we, like Amy, can have those life-changing experiences when the Lord can speak peace to our souls.

Exercises

Ponder the following questions and write down your thoughts.

- What past experiences have you had when the Spirit has borne witness of truth to you as you've studied the scriptures, listened to the words of living prophets and Church leaders, or read the sincere firsthand accounts of figures in Church history?
- What other sources beyond those we've listed in this chapter would you consider to be primary sources, in that they provide maximum opportunity for the Holy Ghost to bear witness of truth?
- How are you doing with this process? Do you feel the Lord is starting to guide you as you seek answers to your questions? Are you having new experiences with the Spirit? Consider writing down the experiences you're having or sharing them with someone else.

Secondary and Critical Sources

In the previous chapter, we identified the scriptures, words of modern prophets and Church leaders, and firsthand accounts as primary sources to include in our study as we seek answers to our sincere questions. We focused on these primary sources first because they cut out the speculation and commentary of other voices and allow direct opportunity for the Spirit to bear witness of truth.

But what about other sources of information beyond those we identified as primary sources? Among all the other voices in the world with something to say about Jesus Christ and The Church of Jesus Christ of Latter-day Saints, surely there must be something there that can help us as we seek answers to our sincere questions. And what about voices that are critical of the Church? How much energy should we invest in listening to those voices? And how do these other sources fit into the process of growing in knowledge of light and truth? We'll discuss these questions in this chapter as we conclude our discussion of the principle of seeking learning by study.

It's worth pausing here for a moment to remind ourselves just how important this is. We are precious. Our time is precious. The most important assets we have to give are our time, energy, and attention. Whatever we give attention to takes away from other things we could invest in. We need to have enough appreciation and respect for ourselves, as divine sons and daughters of God, to be judicious about which voices we give time and attention to. And, as we'll soon learn, just because someone feels that it's important to state their opinion (no matter how loudly), that does not inherently mean that it is worthy of our attention. So how do we determine where to invest our time?

Perhaps we can use an interesting and slightly amusing analogy as we discuss these questions. If you've been grocery shopping and purchased eggs lately, you've probably noticed labeling such as "Grade AA Large Eggs" on your egg cartons. In the United States, the Department of Agriculture (USDA) uses three grades for establishing the quality of eggs sold to consumers. These are grade AA (the highest quality), grade A, and grade B. Have you ever wondered how those grades are determined? For example, what's the difference between a grade AA egg and a grade A egg? The USDA establishes criteria for each grade by considering exterior factors—such as shell cleanliness, stains, integrity, and appearance—and interior factors—such as the air gap inside the egg, the thickness of the white and yolk, the presence of any dark spots, the size of the germ, and so on.[33]

Now, here's what I find interesting: you cannot tell a grade AA egg from a grade A egg or sometimes even a grade B egg just by looking at the outside of it. The true quality of an egg can only be determined by looking at what's inside. But how do you look inside an egg without breaking it open? The only way to determine the highest quality sourced eggs from lesser quality eggs is by holding them up to a light, a technique known as "candling." Light reveals the true quality of an egg.

Now, let's see if we can use this interesting Jeopardy-worthy information about eggs as an analogy for "grading" the quality of information sources we encounter in our search for truth. What "light" can we hold sources up to in order to determine their quality?

Well, certainly one light we can use is the criteria we established for identifying primary sources of information in the previous chapters.

---

33. "United States Standards, Grades, and Weight Classes for Shell Eggs. AMS 56," United States Department of Agriculture, July 20, 2000, https://www.ams.usda.gov/sites/default/files/media/Shell_Egg_Standard%5B1%5D.pdf.

Those criteria are designed to find sources that best align with the divine process of growing in light and truth. In other words, they provide the best opportunity to be exposed to potential truth that the Holy Ghost can bear witness to and that we can exercise our agency to accept or reject. As a reminder of that criteria, when we encounter sources of information, we can ask ourselves the following questions:

- Does this claim to be a source of divine truth?
- Am I studying this source with the intent of giving the Holy Ghost opportunity to bear witness of truth?
- Is this a firsthand source, or is it the commentary and opinion of others?

The primary sources we identified—the scriptures, inspired words of living prophets and Church leaders, and firsthand accounts—are "Grade AA" sources that match our criteria.

But there are many, many other "Grade A" and even "Grade B" sources of truth out there that can aid in our search for answers to our sincere questions.

Secondary Sources

In giving direction to those ordained to the priesthood, the Lord instructed His servants to "preach, teach, expound, [and] exhort" (Doctrine and Covenants 20:46).

The Lord also instructed Emma Smith, one of the most influential women in the Restoration of the Church, "Thou shalt be ordained under [the prophet's] hand to expound scriptures, and to exhort the Church, according as it shall be given thee by my Spirit. For he shall lay his hands upon thee, and thou shalt receive the Holy Ghost, and thy time shall be given to writing, and to learning much" (Doctrine and Covenants 25:7–8).

The Lord has also commanded us to "seek ye diligently and teach one another words of wisdom; yea, seek ye out of the best books words of wisdom; seek learning, even by study and also by faith" (Doctrine and Covenants 88:115).

Through the ages, the Lord has inspired many men and women both inside and outside the Church to preach, teach, expound, exhort, and write as inspired by the Holy Ghost. Many of these individuals have made great personal sacrifices of time to research, study, expand, and articulate their perspective and understanding of truth.

The Lord has also inspired men and women to invest much time in the study of scientific, historical, geographical, and archaeological truths. While these sources cannot and should not replace our primary sources, if we are wise and sincere, the Lord can use these "secondary sources" to expand our understanding, to help us see things from additional perspectives, and to provide a witness of truth through the Holy Ghost.

What are some examples of these secondary sources? They might include the following:

- Inspired writings and commentary of other faithful Christian and religious authors
- The many, many published books and articles of faithful Church members
- Talks given by men and women of high integrity both inside and outside the Church
- BYU devotionals and lectures[34]
- Historical documents and journals such as those found at josephsmithpapers.org
- Collections of information regarding events in Church history that seek to provide a holistic or unbiased perspective
- Websites that sincerely seek to give unbiased, fair perspectives of both the positive and potentially negative elements of gospel topics or Church history
- The perspectives of other Church members who have passed through challenging trials of faith
- Conversations with leaders, friends, and family members
- Well-conducted and verified scientific, archaeological, or historical research

---

34. I've mentioned previously my love for BYU devotionals, many of which are from guest speakers of high integrity from outside the Church who teach truth and offer valuable intellectual and religious perspective.

- Secondhand accounts and commentary of those close to individuals and events in Church history

These are just a few examples of other potential sources of truth that can be instrumental in helping us find answers to our questions. While sources such as these may not necessarily claim to be sources of divine truth, and may contain a significant amount of personal opinion and commentary, certainly the Lord has inspired and guided some of this for our learning and benefit. Hopefully *this* book is worthy of being counted among such sources.

In our trial of faith, we may find that the Lord has divinely inspired someone to create one of these secondary sources specifically to touch our hearts, answer our questions, and rescue us from doubt.

Now, obviously not every source that falls into these categories is divinely inspired or seeks to provide truth. How do we determine which are worthy of our time and attention? What "light" do we hold these up to in order to determine their true quality? Here we again look to Jesus Christ and remember His guidance when He taught, "The Spirit of truth . . . will guide you into all truth" (John 16:13). Similarly, Moroni proclaimed that "by the power of the Holy Ghost ye may know the truth of all things" (Moroni 10:5).

The "candling" method we must use when testing these sources is to hold them up to the light of the Holy Ghost. Again, if our sincere desire is to look unto Christ in every thought, to seek to do His will, and to seek answers by the Spirit to sincere questions, we can trust the Holy Ghost to help us know where to direct our study efforts.

Act in Faith: Identify Your Secondary Sources

Let's continue to act in faith, and continue our exercise from the previous chapter, by identifying potential secondary sources of information to study as we seek answers to our questions through the Holy Ghost.

For each of your sincere questions, prayerfully consider the above list of potential secondary sources. What books, articles, talks, commentary, scientific or historical research, people, conversations, websites, blogs, and so on could you explore as potential sources to study as you seek answers to that particular question? What sources has the

Lord already put in your path? Remember that our intent with these sources is to expose ourselves to potential sources of truth and to provide opportunity for the Holy Ghost to teach us and bear witness of truth to our hearts and minds.

Critical Sources

Obviously, one of the challenges many Church members encounter that can lead to doubt is the large amount of critical and antagonistic commentary that has been created against the Church, its members, and its leaders. Where do these voices fit in the process of our search for truth? And how much of our time and energy should we be spending with such sources?

Some of these voices can also bring added perspective or can help us appreciate and understand other points of view. Elder Gerald N. Lund, renowned author, professor, and former General Authority, in speaking about the much research he had done into the life and character of the Prophet Joseph Smith, stated, "In a way, you can learn a lot about the prophet from his enemies."[35]

Some of these sources can also bring us understanding and empathy for why friends, family members, and others struggle to develop or maintain a testimony of the restored gospel. For some Church members, encountering these sources can prompt them to look to Christ in faith to reinforce and more firmly establish their testimony of the restored gospel.

However, we would be wise to recognize that this collection of sources contains a wide spectrum of information—everything from the well-researched, verified, high-quality commentary of those earnestly seeking the truth to the most baseless, deceitful, destructive opinion of those who have no desire whatsoever to find and live the truth or to lead others to it. And quite honestly, the latter is much more abundant than the former.

---

35. "Gerald N. Lund," Apr. 30, 2012, in *Conversations—A Mormon Channel Original*, podcast, https://broadcast-portal.lds.org/ldsradio/Conversations/2012–04–0380-gerald-n-lund-64k-eng.mp3.

There are two other grade levels for eggs used by the USDA that I didn't mention previously. These grades are "dirty" and "check."[36] Some of these critical sources would certainly fall into the category of being dirty or needing to be checked.

Because of this broad range of quality in this category of sources, the highest degree of wisdom and spiritual discernment is required from us to identify what is truth and what comes from the "father of all lies" (John 8:44). And even for those elements that are true, we desperately need the help of the Holy Ghost to not only recognize them but also to teach us how to process them, how to think about them, and where they fit with our testimony of the restored gospel of Jesus Christ. Knowledge that a seemingly negative piece of information is factual is insufficient. We need the Lord's help to know how to process that information and what we should do about it.

I again reiterate my belief that the primary sources are the essential places to spend our time when we're experiencing a trial of faith. But for those Church members who feel that a study of this category of critical sources must be part of their search for truth, I'd like to suggest including the following considerations as you evaluate whether a source is worthy of your time and how to process it.

Consider the Source

Kevin J. Worthen, former president of Brigham Young University, taught, "Some sources are more reliable than others. In the digital age, everyone has a platform. That has some upside, as it allows voices that were previously unheard to participate in the conversation that is part of the pursuit of truth. At the same time, it allows almost anyone to claim almost anything without the same fact-checking filter that has existed for many mainstream sources in the past."[37]

Some sources demonstrate the responsibility and rigor required to put forth information to the public with integrity. They spend hours researching and verifying their information. They validate their

---

36. "United States Standards, Grades, and Weight Classes for Shell Eggs. AMS 56."

37. Kevin J. Worthen, "The Pursuit of All Truth" (Brigham Young University devotional, Jan. 10, 2017), 5, speeches.byu.edu.

information with multiple sources. They feel a responsibility to be fair, accurate, and honest in what they put forth. Many credible, modern news agencies typically hold themselves to this standard of accountability for what they report.

But in our internet age, there are many, many individuals who are not concerned with whether or not the information or perspective they are putting forth is true. They seek only to persuade others to their point of view and are willing to twist information and facts, omit context, omit other relevant sources, and do whatever it takes to get us to adopt their perspective. Sometimes they are motivated only by a desire for attention or by anger or bitterness. These latter sources, however dramatic or interesting, are likely a waste of our precious time if our objective is to find answers to our own sincere questions and resolve our own doubts.

The Lord has repeatedly explained His use of the law of witnesses to establish truth. He has stated, "In the mouth of two or three witnesses shall every word be established" (2 Corinthians 13:1).

In legal cases, a witness provides firsthand knowledge of the events or subject matter being considered in the case. A judge or jury is then able to evaluate the evidence presented by these witnesses and make a decision as to the outcome of the case. Attorneys and judges are very careful to identify credible witnesses to offer testimony. If a witness is determined not to be credible, their testimony must be thrown out and not considered as part of the determination. Consider this definition of a credible witness given by author John Bouvier:

> A credible witness is one who is competent to give evidence, and is worthy of belief. In deciding upon the credibility of a witness, it is always pertinent to consider [1] whether he is capable of knowing the thing thoroughly about which he testifies. 2. Whether he was actually present at the transaction. 3. Whether he paid sufficient attention to qualify himself to be a reporter of it; and 4. Whether he honestly relates the affair fully as he knows it, without any purpose or desire to deceive, or suppress or add to the truth.[38]

38. "Credible witness," *The Free Dictionary*, accessed Oct. 24, 2023, https://legal-dictionary.thefreedictionary.com/Credible+witness.

So when we encounter a critical or antagonistic source on the internet or in any other venue, it's worth pausing to ask, would this source pass the test of being considered a credible witness on this subject? How much research have they done? Are they giving me factual information or merely cleverly constructed and biased opinion? Have they corroborated their information? What is their motive or intent? Would a reputable organization consider this information to be of high integrity?

Pausing to ask ourselves such questions can allow the Holy Ghost to tell us whether this source is worth our consideration as we seek answers to our sincere questions.

Consider the Intent

The prophet Mormon wrote:

> Wherefore, I show unto you the way to judge; for every thing which inviteth to do good, and to persuade to believe in Christ, is sent forth by the power and gift of Christ; wherefore ye may know with a perfect knowledge it is of God.
>
> But whatsoever thing persuadeth men to do evil, and believe not in Christ, and deny him, and serve not God, then ye may know with a perfect knowledge it is of the devil; for after this manner doth the devil work, for he persuadeth no man to do good, no, not one; neither do his angels; neither do they who subject themselves unto him. (Moroni 7:16–17)

Wisely pausing to consider the intent of the sources we encounter is essential. We might consider asking ourselves the following questions as we evaluate a potential source:

- What is this person's intent? Are they trying to lead me to truth? Are they trying to lead me toward Christ or away from Christ?
- Does this increase or decrease my faith in Christ and His ability to accomplish His work on the earth, even through imperfect servants?
- Does this person's perspective support the process by which God reveals truth and guides His children on earth?

- Are they merely trying to rally support for their ideas or to justify living a particular lifestyle?
- Is this source trying to build me up and give me hope or to tear me down and cause me to doubt and fear?

Give Equal Time and Opportunity

Elder M. Russell Ballard taught, "Never fail to give equal time to the Lord through honest attempts to understand what the Lord has revealed."[39]

While I was serving as a bishop, when Church members would share concerns about their testimony of the gospel, it was not uncommon to discover they had spent the past many days, weeks, months, or even years immersed in the commentary and opinions of voices critical of the Church or its history. Unfortunately, it was also common to discover they hadn't touched the scriptures, or studied the words of living prophets and Church leaders, or gone to the temple, or sometimes even offered a sincere prayer in all that time.

No wonder they were struggling. Such a diet of information is the spiritual equivalent of a physical diet consisting entirely of sugary snacks and soda pop. Imagine what your physical health would be like after weeks and years on such a diet. A spiritual diet devoid of potential sources of divine truth and the words of Christ will eventually lead anyone to doubt, confusion, anxiety, and unhappiness.

The principle of giving equal time means that we give as much opportunity to the Lord to teach us as we're giving to the voices of opinion to persuade our thinking. And it also means giving equal or fair consideration.

What does giving equal time look like? If we're just starting to study a particular topic, it may look like balancing the amount of time we're giving to detracting voices with at least an equivalent number of hours given to the scriptures, words of living prophets, firsthand accounts, and positive commentary of the restored gospel.

However, if we've recently been spending the vast majority of our time studying these critical sources, we may need to take a break. If

---

39. M. Russell Ballard, "To Whom Shall We Go?," *Ensign*, Nov. 2016, 91.

we've been immersed for a long period of time in anti-Church material, giving equal time may mean that it's time to give those voices a rest and now give that same opportunity back to the Lord to teach us through the Spirit. We should make a commitment to ourselves to identify relevant primary sources and high-quality secondary sources and immerse ourselves in those with the same investment we've been making in the opposing material. We owe that much to ourselves out of respect for how precious our time and mindshare are.

This is in no way putting blinders on or ignoring information. Rather, this is being responsible and demonstrating integrity in our search for truth. It's effectively going to the Lord and saying, "I've gone and read and studied all this other stuff. I'm now going back to the basics to try to cut out the earthly commentary."

It's worth pausing to ask ourselves, "Have I given fair and equal opportunity to the primary and secondary sources of truth as I've given to the critical voices?"

Know Our Limits

As a bishop, I visited with a very faithful brother who had held many leadership positions in the Church. Amidst our other topics of conversation, he mentioned that he'd developed some concerns about a few topics related to Church history. He indicated he was doing a little research and trying to be very careful and balanced in his study. I offered my help and let him know I was willing to discuss these things any time he felt the need.

When we next met, I casually asked how things were going with his concerns. He indicated that he'd decided to put those concerns on a shelf for now, and that he didn't feel like he was prepared to give them attention at that time.

I remember respecting how wisely this faithful brother approached his concerns, knowing his own limitations and how much energy to give them. Several months later, when we met again, he indicated that those matters were no longer of concern to him. The Spirit had taught him what he needed to know during the intervening months.

Sometimes we need to check our own readiness and capability to tackle a thorny topic. We're all busy. We have limited time and energy to invest in our education, career, family, callings, and gospel study.

The Spirit can tell us when it's okay to put our concerns on a shelf to be dealt with at a later time. Sometimes the concern isn't as urgent or pressing as it may presently seem. We typically run very little risk by giving the Spirit more time to speak to our hearts and minds on a subject before diving into a deep study on a concern.

Brother Michael Otterson, a convert to the Church and the former managing director of public affairs for the Church, shared his experience of sifting through a lot of anti-Church material when he was first introduced to the Church in Liverpool, England. At that time, desiring to learn as much as possible, he went to the Liverpool library and checked out and read all thirty-three books the library had about the "Mormon Church." Of those thirty-three books, one was the Book of Mormon, one was a positive perspective on the Church written by a nonmember, and the other thirty-one books were anti-Mormon perspectives.

Brother Otterson stated, "Obviously I got through that, and I found most of the material patently absurd, frankly. And I didn't have any trouble finding counter-arguments to most of it."[40]

Now, here I think it's worth noting that Brother Otterson is a journalist by profession, and his training, both through education and career experience, was to identify and separate fact from fiction through rigorous research. Most of us do not have that same background and training and may more easily be drawn into someone's arguments without the mental processes in place to know how to validate those arguments. It's wise for us to be aware of our own capabilities and limitations here.

However, what Brother Otterson subsequently stated is indeed applicable to all of us: "One thing I learned is that, if you are properly anchored in the gospel, if you have that spiritual conversion, that spiritual testimony, then you can see all of this other material in its perspective and context."[41]

---

40. "Michael Otterson - Public Affairs," July 2, 2012, in *Conversations—A Mormon Channel Original*, podcast, https://broadcast-portal.lds.org/ldsradio/Conversations/2012–07–0420-michael-otterson-public-affairs-64k-eng.mp3.

41. "Michael Otterson - Public Affairs."

The Spirit can tell us where we stand in regard to our preparation and ability to properly navigate certain critical material. If the Spirit prompts us that perhaps we're not prepared to discern truth from error in a particularly sophisticated or enticing argument, it's not an act of fear to wisely give heed to those promptings and instead direct our study to other areas as guided by the Spirit. This is one way of looking to Christ in our study.

Listen to the Voice of the Spirit

After all the other considerations we make when approaching sources critical of the Church, the single most important, again, is to look to Christ and trust in His counsel that "the Spirit of truth . . . will guide you into all truth" (John 16:13).

The Holy Ghost can tell us in our hearts and our minds if the material we are taking in comes from the Lord or is going to be beneficial in our personal search for truth. His voice trumps all others, and we will be greatly blessed as we learn to recognize it.

As a missionary in Costa Rica, I remember being invited into a home where we'd hoped to share the gospel. The homeowner was kind and gracious. After a few minutes of casual conversation, he placed a book in my hands. Immediately, before I read the cover or opened the book, I felt a dark, almost sick feeling come over me. I didn't know at that moment what the book contained, but there was a distinct feeling that this was not something I wanted to be involved in. And it wasn't a feeling of fear but rather of wise warning. I opened the book and began to thumb through its pages, glancing here and there at some of the arguments—it was clearly an anti-Mormon book. And the impression I got from the Spirit was that this was not from God and that He did not want me to investigate it further.

I have a firm witness that we are not left alone to sift through all the voices out there to know who we should listen to. If we're sincerely seeking to do the right thing and truly desire to be led to truth, we can rely on the Holy Ghost to direct us to those sources of study where the Lord wants us to spend our time.

Act in Faith: Test Critical Sources

Before we conclude this principle of seeking learning by study, let's pause for a moment to practice what we've just discussed. If you've been encountering sources that are critical of the Church, try evaluating them against the considerations we've outlined above. For each source, consider asking yourself these questions:

- Is this a credible source? Does it demonstrate responsibility and integrity in the arguments it is making and the outcomes it may produce?
- What is the source's intent? Is the source seeking to lead me to truth and to Christ or away from Him? Is it motivated by self-interest, anger, fear, or hatred?
- Am I giving fair and equal opportunity to the primary and secondary sources of information, and for the Lord to bear witness of those sources?
- What are my own limits? How prepared am I to properly research and discern truth from error in this source? Is this something I should defer until later?
- What is the Holy Ghost trying to tell me about this source? Is this a source I should be studying now, or is the Spirit trying to tell me to spend my time elsewhere?

Summary: Seek Learning by Study

We've spent the last three chapters discussing the essential principle of seeking learning by study. We've learned that growing in a knowledge of light and truth is integral to who we are as sons and daughters of God. Truth is part of our spiritual makeup, and we are driven to acquire it. A fulness of joy will come as we grow in light and truth until we possess and live a fulness of truth. We've discussed the divine process by which we grow in light and truth and the sources of opposition we encounter in that process. We've established criteria for identifying sources most likely to facilitate and accelerate that process. Using those criteria, we identified three categories of "primary sources" to include in our study. We've acted in faith to identify sources specific to our personal questions. We've discussed other great secondary sources of study in our search for truth. And we've shared some important considerations to make when we study or encounter sources that are negative or critical of the Church.

As we've been deliberately acting in faith, I hope you are feeling the Spirit guide you in seeking out the sources that will bring you the answers, experiences, and peace you seek. I give my personal witness that as we invest our precious time in studying the most important sources, we can have personal life-changing experiences with our Heavenly Father, our Savior, and the Holy Ghost. I believe we will feel of their love for us and discover they've gone out of Their way to create a gospel study plan specifically for us. The Lord is eager to calm our fears, bring peace to our hearts, and guide us to answers to our sincere questions through a study of truth.

Sources, Mercy, and a Witness

Before moving on to the next principle, I feel to pause here to reflect back on our second principle, which was Moroni's plea to "remember how merciful the Lord hath been" (Moroni 10:3). I'd like to share one element of my own personal witness of God's mercy as it has come through the study of primary sources.

A common source of doubt for many Church members comes in the form of questions surrounding the life of the Prophet Joseph Smith. That's not surprising given challenging topics such as plural marriage or the fact that it is simply difficult to develop a clear perspective of facts and events based on limited historical evidence and commentary. And certainly anyone who embarks on a serious study of Church history will find ample commentary that is critical of the Prophet and early Church leaders.

One of the contributions to my witness of the divine calling of the Prophet Joseph Smith comes from historical accounts from several primary sources that demonstrate God's pattern of intentionally working through the imperfections of His servants. I would like to share one element of my personal witness resulting from my own sincere study efforts.

Most Church members are familiar with the account of the 116 manuscript pages translated from the Book of Mormon that were lost by Joseph Smith and Martin Harris. However, there are details surrounding that account that strengthen my faith in the Savior and His ability to foresee and compensate for the weaknesses and mistakes of His servants while also allowing for their growth and learning. This account also helps me to have empathy for those imperfect men and women who, like all of us, are sometimes called upon to fill shoes that are often far too big for them.

In September 1827, Joseph Smith received the gold plates containing the record of the Book of Mormon from the angel Moroni (see Joseph Smith—History 1:59). At that time, Joseph and his wife Emma were living at the Smith family home in Palmyra, New York. Over the next several months, attempts to steal the plates from the Smith family became increasingly frequent and violent. In December 1827, Joseph and Emma moved to the home of her parents in Harmony, Pennsylvania, where the plates could be kept safe and the work of translating the Book of Mormon could be accomplished. Emma was also pregnant with their first child.

For a little perspective, Joseph was twenty-two years old, and Emma was twenty-three. In the Church today, we would refer to them as "young adults," just a few years older than most returning missionaries.

Emma initially served as Joseph's scribe in the early months of 1828. Between April and June, Joseph worked on the translation, with Martin Harris acting as his primary scribe.[42] By mid-June, 116 pages of manuscript were complete. Martin implored Joseph to allow him to carry the manuscript home to Palmyra where he could show his wife and others the results of their work in hopes of providing evidence of its truthfulness.

Joseph importuned the Lord three times to ask if Martin could take the manuscript, and only upon the last inquiry did the Lord give consent under condition that Martin show the pages to only five named individuals, to which Martin agreed under written commitment.

If the dates we have are correct, Martin left Joseph on June 14, 1828. The very next day, June 15, Emma gave birth to their first child. The baby boy, who they named Alvin after Joseph's deceased brother,

---

42. See History, 1838–1856 [Manuscript History of the Church], volume A-1 [23 December 1805–30 August 1834], 9, josephsmithpapers.org.

died just a few hours later.[43] For several weeks, Emma was so low that it was feared she too might pass away, and Joseph dared not leave her side. As Emma finally began to recover, Joseph's anxiety shifted to another problem: Martin had not returned with the manuscript, and Joseph had heard nothing from him since his departure. Joseph did not dare mention his concerns to Emma given her physical and emotional state. Ultimately, it was Emma—whose personal sacrifice, effort, and handwriting were also represented in those missing pages—who expressed her concern and strongly encouraged Joseph to return to Palmyra to resolve the situation.

Joseph took the first available stagecoach to Palmyra, 155 miles away, then walked through the night, accompanied by a concerned stranger, to arrive at his parents' home. After taking some food, Joseph requested the family to send for Martin to come. After a long delay, Martin finally arrived looking very distressed.

The remainder of the account can only be done justice by hearing it directly from the firsthand source as recorded by Joseph's mother, Lucy Mack Smith:

> Mr. Harris pressed his hands upon his temples, and cried out in a tone of deep anguish, "Oh, I have lost my soul! I have lost my soul!"
>
> Joseph who had not expressed his fears till now, sprang from the table, exclaiming, "Martin, have you lost that manuscript? Have you broken your oath, and brought down condemnation upon my head as well as your own?"
>
> "Yes; it is gone," replied Martin, "and I know not where."
>
> "Oh, my God!" said Joseph, clinching his hands. "All is lost! all is lost! What shall I do? I have sinned—it is I who tempted the wrath of God. I should have been satisfied with the first answer which I received from the Lord; for he told me that it was not safe to let the writing go out of my possession." He wept and groaned, and walked the floor continually.
>
> At length he told Martin to go back and search again.
>
> "No"; said Martin, "it is all in vain; for I have ripped open beds and pillows; and I know it is not there."

43. See History, 1838–1856 [Manuscript History of the Church], volume A-1 [23 December 1805–30 August 1834], 9, josephsmithpapers.org.

> "Then must I," said Joseph, "return with such a tale as this? I dare not do it. And how shall I appear before the Lord? Of what rebuke am I not worthy from the angel of the Most High?" . . .
>
> I besought him not to mourn so, for perhaps the Lord would forgive him, after a short season of humiliation and repentance. But what could I do to comfort him, when he saw all the family in the same situation of mind as himself; for sobs and groans, and the most bitter lamentations filled the house. However, Joseph was more distressed than the rest, as he better understood the consequences of disobedience. And he continued pacing back and forth, meantime weeping and grieving, until about sunset, when, by persuasion, he took a little nourishment.
>
> The next morning, he set out for home. We parted with heavy hearts, for it now appeared that all which we had so fondly anticipated, and which had been the source of so much secret gratification, had in a moment fled, and fled forever.[44]

I may not be able to personally relate to Joseph Smith as the prophet who the Lord called to restore His Church, or who saw God the Father and Jesus Christ, or who translated an ancient record through revelation, or who communicated with angels from heaven. But I can certainly relate to a very young husband and father, under crushing personal stress, who the Lord asked to do something and who found that his performance, quite honestly, just wasn't good enough. And I can relate to the feeling that perhaps some careless, fearful action on my part may have jeopardized the future God had planned for me and those I love. I know that feeling.

If the story ended there, it truly would be heartbreaking. The gift and ability to translate were taken from Joseph for a time (see Doctrine and Covenants 3:14). But perhaps the most searing chastisement of all came in the words of the Lord Himself to Joseph as they are publicly preserved for all generations to witness in Doctrine and Covenants 3. You might try putting yourself in Joseph's shoes and imagine what it may have felt like to receive these words from the Lord:

---

44. Lucy Mack Smith, *History of Joseph Smith by His Mother*, ed. Preston Nibley (1958), 125–29.

> For although a man may have many revelations, and have power to do many mighty works, yet if he boasts in his own strength, and sets at naught the counsels of God, and follows after the dictates of his own will and carnal desires, he must fall and incur the vengeance of a just God upon him.
>
> Behold, you have been entrusted with these things, but how strict were your commandments; and remember also the promises which were made to you, if you did not transgress them.
>
> And behold, how oft you have transgressed the commandments and the laws of God, and have gone on in the persuasions of men.
>
> For, behold, you should not have feared man more than God. Although men set at naught the counsels of God, and despise his words—
>
> Yet you should have been faithful; and he would have extended his arm and supported you against all the fiery darts of the adversary; and he would have been with you in every time of trouble.
>
> Behold, thou art Joseph, and thou wast chosen to do the work of the Lord, but because of transgression, if thou art not aware thou wilt fall. (Doctrine and Covenants 3:5–9)

Those words surely must have cut Joseph to the core, and all this came on top of the other financial, physical, and emotional challenges that Joseph and Emma were experiencing.

The Lord, demonstrating His mercy for His servants, and providing perhaps the perfect tie-in to Moroni's plea to us to remember God's mercy, followed His chastisement to Joseph with these words of forgiveness and hope: "But remember, God is merciful; therefore, repent of that which thou hast done which is contrary to the commandment which I gave you, and thou art still chosen, and art again called to the work" (Doctrine and Covenants 3:10).

We subsequently learn that the Lord had foreseen and planned for Joseph's difficult learning experience (see Doctrine and Covenants 10; Words of Mormon 1:1–7). Some of the most beautiful doctrines regarding the Atonement of Christ and the plan of salvation were given to us in the Book of Mormon because of those lost 116 pages. Had Joseph and Martin not made this mistake, we might never have received the writings of Nephi, or the allegory of the olive tree as included by Jacob (see Jacob 5), or Lehi's teachings about agency and opposition (2 Nephi 2), or Enos's account of receiving a remission of his sins (see Enos 1). Clearly the Lord provisioned for this experience.

Regarding this very matter, the Lord said, "The works, and the designs, and the purposes of God cannot be frustrated, neither can they come to naught. . . . Remember, remember that it is not the work of God that is frustrated, but the work of men" (Doctrine and Covenants 3:1, 3).

This account from sources in Church history strengthens my faith in Christ. It bears witness to me of His loving patience and willingness to let us grow, forgive us for our mistakes, and allow us to participate in His work despite our failings and imperfections. It gives me confidence that God is always at the helm and that we don't need to worry about His ability to lead His Church.

Elder Neil L. Andersen gave the following counsel to those who wrestle with questions regarding the Prophet Joseph Smith: "To those of faith who, looking through the colored glasses of the 21st century, honestly question events or statements of the Prophet Joseph from nearly 200 years ago, may I share some friendly advice: For now, give Brother Joseph a break! In a future day, you will have 100 times more information than from all of today's search engines combined, and it will come from our all-knowing Father in Heaven."[45]

As I reflect on Joseph's experience, I feel tender empathy and admiration for the humility and faith of the young Prophet, his faithful wife Emma, Martin Harris, the Smith family, and all others who were called to help restore the Church. And with that empathy, and God's mercy in mind, I find myself less inclined to judge them as they struggled to discover and accomplish the Lord's will in the face of their own glaring imperfections. In other words, I feel inclined to "give Brother Joseph a break."

"Could I have done any better had I been in their shoes?" I ask myself. I don't think so. "Would a man seeking to deceive the world be so inclined to put this failed experience on public display for all future generations to see?" My heart tells me no.

---

45. Neil L. Andersen, "Faith Is Not by Chance, but by Choice," *Ensign*, Nov. 2015, 66.

Recall once again the experience of my friend Amy, whose questions were indeed surrounding reported events in the life of Joseph Smith. Amy was able to come to peace with her concerns as she experienced God's mercy in her own life. "I realized that I don't need to be their judge," she stated. "I may not understand their actions, but their experiences don't affect my testimony of the things that I know to be true."

If we can develop the same perspective and mercy that Amy demonstrated—which Elder Anderson spoke of and which Moroni pleads with us to remember—we can draw closer to Christ and give ourselves the space and time we need in order to seek and receive the witness of the Holy Ghost regarding the truths that matter most.

I am so grateful for these primary sources of information: the account of Joseph's mother, the revelations from the Lord found in the Doctrine and Covenants, the historical data regarding Joseph and Emma's family circumstances, and the counsel of living prophets and apostles. These sources have given me the opportunity for the Holy Ghost to teach me and strengthen my testimony of the Prophet and the Lord's ability to guide His church despite our imperfections.

Exercises

Ponder the following questions and write down your thoughts.

- What feelings do you have as you consider Joseph Smith's experience as shared in this chapter and the Lord's chastisement of Joseph captured in Doctrine and Covenants 3?
- What do you learn about God's mercy from this experience?

Principle 7: Prayer

"I have been driven many times upon my knees by the overwhelming conviction that I had nowhere else to go. My own wisdom and that of all about me seemed insufficient for that day." (Abraham Lincoln)[46]

My companion and I had been teaching Luciana the missionary discussions for several months. Luciana was a very intelligent, bright young woman living in the home of a local Church member while attending a university in Costa Rica. Luciana had fantastic questions, and she'd been diligent in fulfilling the reading assignments we'd given her in the Book of Mormon. She'd also attended church a number of times. But she still hadn't made the decision to be baptized. My companion and I were puzzled because we felt certain she'd received many spiritual confirmations from the Holy Ghost that what we were sharing was true. We'd certainly felt the presence of the Spirit many times in our lessons with her. We began to wonder if maybe there wasn't much more we could do to help her, and we considered concluding our lessons. We decided to hold one last lesson with her.

My companion and I prayed to know what to discuss with Luciana. We prayed before we entered her home to share the message we'd prepared. And then we asked Luciana to pray before we

---

46. Noah Brooks, *Lincoln Observed: The Civil War Dispatches of Noah Brooks*, ed. Michael Burlingame (Baltimore, MD: Johns Hopkins University Press, 1998), 210.

began our lesson. In that prayer, Luciana asked to know if what we had been teaching her was true. It was a very simple but very sincere prayer. It was not the rushed routine prayer we often utter. Her words were halting and thoughtful, and she really was speaking directly to our Heavenly Father, sharing her feelings and genuinely asking for answers.

We showed a simple Church video and then shared a few brief scriptures about hearing the voice of the Holy Ghost. And then, quite suddenly, the Holy Ghost entered the room in a very recognizable way, and Luciana began to cry (really to weep) uncontrollably. This was completely uncharacteristic of this usually composed, intellectual young woman. My companion and I felt compelled to be still and silent. There was a feeling of love, peace, comfort, and witness in the room. Luciana's tears continued for about two minutes. Apologizing, she regained her composure, apologized, and said, "I think I may have just received my answer." She tried to describe what she'd felt. Luciana again closed the meeting with prayer, telling our Heavenly Father what she'd just experienced and asking Him to let her know if that was her answer.

It would be another month of teaching and resolving questions and concerns before Luciana would make the decision to be baptized. When she did make that decision, she wanted to act as soon as possible. There were many elements in Luciana's gaining a witness of the restored gospel and the Book of Mormon, but that personal experience she had with the Holy Ghost as a result of her sincere prayer was foundational. That experience was something my companion and I could never provide her.

Prayer is our next principle. In this chapter, we'll talk about how to pray for what we really need when we're wrestling with doubt and seeking answers to our sincere questions. I hope something here makes a difference for you in how you approach our Heavenly Father as you seek answers to the questions of your soul.

Moroni's Promise

The second principle we discussed was motivated by Moroni's plea to us to remember how merciful God is with His children and has been since the days of Adam. Moroni's very next plea to us in the following verse reads, "And when ye shall receive these things, I would exhort you that ye would ask God, the Eternal Father, in the name of Christ, if these things are not true; and if ye shall ask with a sincere heart, with real intent, having faith in Christ, he will manifest the truth of it unto you, by the power of the Holy Ghost" (Moroni 10:4).

In all our personal efforts in our search for truth—in remembering God's mercy, remembering our past spiritual experiences, identifying our doubts and replacing them with sincere questions, reaching out to priesthood leaders for help, and engaging in sincere gospel study—through all of this, perhaps the single most important thing we can do is to connect directly with the source of all truth, our Heavenly Father, through sincere, heartfelt prayer.

This probably seems obvious, and yet it is so common to find that members who are struggling with their testimonies are also having a hard time praying or perhaps haven't been praying for some time. Why is this? Why is it that in a trial of faith, when we would seemingly need to communicate with our Heavenly Father the most, we may begin to distance ourselves from prayer? Here are a few possible reasons you may have experienced.

Concerns about our own worthiness:

- We may struggle to feel the Lord's love for us or question His desires to hear from us or answer our prayers.
- We may have an incorrect perception of God and His attributes.
- We may feel guilty for doubts we've been experiencing.
- We may feel we're unworthy to approach the Lord in prayer because of our own mistakes and sins.

Concerns about our ability to receive answers:

- We may question our own ability to recognize answers to prayer, worrying that we may simply further confuse ourselves.

- We may have had past experiences when we felt we didn't receive answers to prayer or when the answer we received didn't lead to the result we'd hoped for.
- We may be afraid of receiving answers from the Lord because of the implications to act that such answers might bring.
- Our wrestle with doubt may have us questioning our entire religious background, including prayer or the existence of God.

Concerns regarding our desire to pray:

- We may be wrestling with our agency and desires to live life in a way contrary to what we think the Lord would have us do.
- We may already know the answer to the question and are afraid to acknowledge that answer.
- We may have fallen out of the habit of praying and instead have developed the pattern of looking to the voices of the world for wisdom.
- We may not know what to pray for as we wrestle with doubt.

Worthy to Pray

The first category of concerns listed above have to deal with questions about our own worthiness to pray or our Heavenly Father's desire to answer our prayers,

In the Bible Dictionary, on the topic of "Prayer," we read, "As soon as we learn the true relationship in which we stand toward God (namely, God is our Father, and we are His children), then at once prayer becomes natural and instinctive on our part. Many of the so-called difficulties about prayer arise from forgetting this relationship."

In discussing God's mercy, we talked about the Savior's unfailing love for us and His overwhelming desire to save us. We discussed how He desperately desires all of God's children to come unto Him, especially those who are lost in sin. "Come unto me ye ends of the earth," the Savior said, "and be saved" (3 Nephi 9:22).

We've also mentioned the Lord's frequent repetition of this invitation: "Ask, and it shall be given you; seek, and ye shall find; knock, and it shall be opened unto you: For every one that asketh receiveth; and he that seeketh findeth; and to him that knocketh it shall be opened" (Matthew 7:7–8).

No matter where we stand in our current level of obedience to the gospel, regardless of how imperfect we are or how many mistakes we've made or are currently making, our Heavenly Father longs to hear from us. He stands ready to receive our sincere, heartfelt prayers.

My wife and I have four beautiful, wonderful children. Each one of them is completely unique from the others. It is true that sometimes their actions frustrate and annoy me. And sometimes I spend days, weeks, or months worrying about them, especially the teenagers. But as imperfect as I am, and no matter what they do, if any of my children were ever to come to me in sincerity seeking help, comfort, love, or guidance, there is nothing they have ever done or could ever do that would prevent me from doing everything in my power to help them and make them feel loved. And my heart would be especially turned toward a child who is in the middle of serious struggle. I am certain that our Heavenly Father feels the same about us.

There is no level of worthiness required to reach out to our Heavenly Father when we are sincerely seeking His help. It is my experience that when we're struggling, He's been there waiting, planning, and preparing for the moment that we'll choose to come to Him so that He can intervene in our lives and lead us to a better place.

An Act of Faith

The second category of concerns consists of doubts about our ability to receive answers to prayer or the effectiveness or value of prayer. When Nephi's brothers were struggling to understand symbolic truths that their father Lehi had shared with them, Nephi asked them, "Have ye inquired of the Lord?" (1 Nephi 15:8). Nephi was saddened when his brothers responded, "We have not; for the Lord maketh no such thing known unto us" (1 Nephi 15:9). They effectively determined, "We haven't prayed because the Lord doesn't answer us when we pray."

Nephi's brother's allowed doubt to prevent them from doing the work that would lead to the result they were seeking—in other words, their doubt prevented them from acting in faith. Like most of the other principles we've discussed, prayer is a form of work. Prayer is action that we take to prepare our hearts to receive truth and demonstrate to our Heavenly Father that we are desirous and willing to receive His will.

Will the Lord hear my prayer? Will He answer my prayer? Will I be able to recognize an answer? These are all normal concerns that most of us experience at some point. Our Heavenly Father is wise and all-knowing. Instead of fearing our ability to receive answers, we can instead choose to demonstrate trust in *His* ability to answer our prayers in a way that we can recognize. We can replace our fears with faith in God's ability to answer us in the way He knows we need.

The prophet Nephi taught, "For if ye would hearken unto the Spirit which teacheth a man to pray, ye would know that ye must pray; for the evil spirit teacheth not a man to pray, but teacheth him that he must not pray" (2 Nephi 32:8).

If there are voices telling us that we are not worthy to pray, or that our Heavenly Father does not want to hear from us, or that we won't be able to receive or distinguish an answer, please choose to push those voices aside, knowing that they are not coming from the Holy Ghost or from our Heavenly Father. They are, most likely, yet another attempt of the adversary to separate us from what we most need right now: the saving grace of a Heavenly Father who loves us.

What Should We Pray For?

Many of us typically live far below our privilege when it comes to prayer. Years of offering quick mealtime and bedtime prayers filled with routine requests for simple blessings are not a terrible thing, but perhaps it's not ideal training when it comes to seeking help with the most important questions of the soul.

So when we're wrestling with doubt or seeking answers to our sincere questions, what should we pray for? How do we pray? Of course, there is no exact script or recipe for what our dialogue with our Heavenly Father should look like. But as we prepare to take our questions and concerns to our Heavenly Father, we can consider including the following elements.

Share Our Sincere Feelings

If we were to have a face-to-face, sit-down, one-on-one interview with our Heavenly Father, perhaps one of the first things He would ask is "How are you doing? Tell me how things are going for you."

One of the most important things we can do when going through a trial of faith is to open up and share our struggles, thoughts, and feelings with Him. Instead of just asking for blessings or information, we should explain to our Heavenly Father what we're going through.

We can tell Him how we've been feeling. We can tell Him we're angry, upset, afraid, worried, alone, confused, conflicted, or insecure. We can even vent our frustrations at Him if needed. He's a very secure and all-powerful, loving God. He can handle it.

In order for us to connect with our Heavenly Father, it's important that we be very open and honest with Him about how we're feeling.

State the Problem

We can share with the Lord the problem that we're struggling with. Explain what it is that you've encountered that's caused you to feel what you're feeling. How did you arrive at this moment?

It might look something like this: "Father, I encountered this new information about Church history that I never knew before, and now I'm struggling to understand or believe . . ."

As part of our exercise of converting doubts into questions, we also identified the underlying fears associated with our doubts. As we explain our doubts and concerns, it's also appropriate to openly share our fears with the Lord.

Share the Work We Have Done

We can share with the Lord the work we've already done in our search for answers. What have you read, listened to, or watched as you've tried to figure this out, and how have those sources made you feel? What changes are you trying to make in your life?

We can tell Him the ideas we've had and what resources we've utilized thus far in our search for truth. We can tell Him what we're thinking or feeling about that information.

Ask Forgiveness

We're going to talk more about this in the next principle, but I'll touch briefly on it here. As we bring our doubts and questions to our Heavenly Father, we're likely to become very aware of our own sins and shortcomings. Not only is that okay, but it's a wonderful blessing. We should absolutely not let that turn us away from the Lord.

We can be honest with Him about what we've done or how we feel about ourselves. We can tell Him we're sorry and ask forgiveness for our sins: for saying things we shouldn't have said, for not coming to Him sooner, for not living up to our own expectations, for choices we regret, for being unkind in our words or thoughts toward His children, or for abandoning things we knew were true.

As we'll discuss more, that honesty with ourselves and with our Heavenly Father is an essential step in clearing a place in our hearts and minds so that the Spirit can speak to us.

Ask to Feel His Love

John the Apostle wrote, "There is no fear in love; but perfect love casteth out fear" (1 John 4:18).

This world is difficult. It can beat us down. It's easy to get lost in the many voices telling us who we are and what we should be. The love of our heavenly parents can often cast out all fear and cut through confusion and doubt faster than any other experience. If it's been some time since you've felt that love, please consider asking the Lord, "Can you help me feel your love for me?"

There is no way I can express in writing the way our Heavenly Father feels for us. It's something that can only be experienced and felt individually. But in case you're having a hard time hearing His voice, the answer to the question "Do you love me?" is an overwhelming, resounding YES! I believe our Father would want to say something like this: "More than you can ever know. More than you can understand or take in. No matter what you've done, no matter where you go, no matter what happens to you, no matter what other voices lead you to believe, I love you with a love that is unending and unchanging. I'm here ready to help you, and my love is enough to bring you back from the darkest abyss if you'll let me." If we're ever doubting how our Father feels about us, we can ask Him directly.

Similarly, if our doubts have led us to develop hard feelings toward others—toward prophets, Church leaders, or any other of God's children—it's worth asking the Lord, "Can you help me feel your love for them?"

And if our doubts include conflicted feelings of concern for a loved one—a son or daughter, father or mother, grandson or granddaughter, or a dear friend—it is absolutely appropriate to ask the Lord to help us feel His love for them and to help them feel that love also.

Ask Our Sincere Questions

Having done all this work to identify the most important questions of our soul, prayer is now our opportunity to ask those sincere questions to Him directly and listen in the ensuing moments, hours, days, and weeks to the repeated impressions, feelings, and thoughts that come to us.

Ask for Guidance

Although we may have done a lot of our own work in seeking answers to our questions, the Lord likely has some other ideas to share with us. "What would you like me to do? Who should I talk to? Is there anything I should read, listen to, or study? Can you guide me to the resources I need to get through this?" These are all great questions we can and should ask our Heavenly Father as we counsel with Him in prayer.

Ask Him to Teach You

Janette wrestled mightily with anxiety and perfectionism, largely resulting from experiences in her childhood. Her experience and family relationships made it difficult for her to feel God's love for her. She had an incorrect perception of herself and how the Lord felt about her. As we counseled together, I invited her to ask the Lord these questions in her prayers: "Can you help me understand how you feel about me? Can you teach me how I should think and feel about myself? Can you teach me to recognize when I'm thinking or feeling something about myself that's not true?"

"I've never thought to pray that way before," Janette said. "I've always asked for blessings but never for the Lord to teach me how to think." This adjustment in her approach completely changed things for Janette as the Lord gradually taught her how to change her thinking.

In Proverbs, we read, "Wisdom is the principal thing; therefore get wisdom: and with all thy getting get understanding" (Proverbs 4:7).

Recall that the process of growing in light and truth is meant to change our nature: to transform us and not merely inform us. Sometimes what we most need in that process is not additional facts or information. Sometimes what we really need is increased understanding, wisdom, and perspective. Sometimes what we really need is a change of heart. If we'll ask, the Lord can teach us how to think and how to feel about the concerns we have or the information we've encountered.

So it's worth asking the Lord questions like these: "Can you teach me how to think and feel about this? How do you feel about it? How do you think I should feel about this? Am I asking the right questions? Should I be asking a different question? Should I be focused on something else?"

Pray with Real Intent

Moroni's request indicates we should "ask with a sincere heart, with real intent, having faith in Christ" (Moroni 10:4). In Principle 3, we talked about what it means to identify sincere questions and to ask with real intent. It means that we approach the Lord with a sincere willingness to follow the counsel He gives us. It means we approach Him with intent to act.

I return again to one of my favorite examples of sincere prayer found in the Book of Mormon. Having just been taught the gospel of Jesus Christ by the great missionary Aaron, the Lamanite king desired to know what he needed to do to receive a witness that those things were true. Aaron told him he needed to pray and ask God. Here is the prayer the king offered:

> And it came to pass that when Aaron had said these words, the king did bow down before the Lord, upon his knees; yea, even he did prostrate himself upon the earth, and cried mightily, saying:
>
> O God, Aaron hath told me that there is a God; and if there is a God, and if thou art God, wilt thou make thyself known unto me, and I will give away all my sins to know thee, and that I may be raised from the dead, and be saved at the last day. (Alma 22:17–18)

How's that for sincerity and real intent? The king came to the Lord knowing very little, but he was willing to do whatever was necessary to know the Lord. What are we willing to do if the Lord answers our prayers? Are we willing to change our thinking? Are we willing to repent and give away all our sins? Are we willing to follow the example of our Savior and stand apart from social and political norms if that's what is required?

As we speak to our Heavenly Father, we can tell Him how we're feeling about these things, and we can tell Him what we're willing to do to receive the answers we're seeking.

Act in Faith: Pray

Prayer is an essential element in the process of resolving our doubts, finding answers to our questions, and developing that personal relationship with our Heavenly Father and Savior that we desperately need.

I hope something in this chapter has been helpful as we prepare to converse with our Heavenly Father regarding our concerns and sincere questions. As you include prayer in your search for truth, consider the elements we discussed in this chapter of sharing your sincere feelings, explaining the problem you're wrestling with, sharing the work you've done to understand and learn, seeking the Lord's forgiveness, asking to feel His love for you, asking your sincere questions, seeking His guidance, asking Him to teach you and change you, and having real intent to act on the answers you receive.

You might make a list of the things you most want to include in your prayers. Then make a plan. Find a quiet place where you can devote the time and attention you need. Commit to making this a regular part of your daily routine as you work through your concerns and seek answers to your questions. The answers to our prayers come in different ways, but I give my witness that they do come. Our Heavenly Father eagerly desires to hear your voice and provide the help you sincerely seek.

Exercises

Ponder the following questions and write down your thoughts.

- What spiritual experiences have you had through prayer? What answers have you received through prayer in your life?
- Study the topic of prayer as found in the Bible Dictionary. What do you learn about prayer as you ponder that definition and the associated scripture references?
- For some people, thoughts and feelings come more clearly and poignantly while writing rather than speaking. If you are one of those individuals, consider using an electronic device or pen and paper to write your thoughts and feelings as you pray.

Principle 8: Repentance

"So often we are haunted not only with the question of whether we have gone far enough in our own religious experience but also whether we can rely on some things we have previously trusted. Acids eat away at us. Sometimes it is the taunting of other voices; but sometimes it is nothing more profound than our own sins and weaknesses, and the betrayals of the best in ourselves. Doubt naturally follows."
—Truman G. Madsen[47]

Andrew was a wonderful young man from a faithful Latter-day Saint family. He had faithfully served a devoted mission, sharing the gospel of Christ with others. After returning from his mission, he again began to court his lovely girlfriend, also a faithful member of the Church. As can happen all too often, they weren't careful enough with their physical affections toward each other. They let things go too far. And this young, faithful returned missionary found himself experiencing the feelings of guilt that come with having committed serious sin.

About eighteen months later, he sat in front of his bishop confessing what had happened.

"Andrew, I'm so glad you decided to come," his bishop said. "Why didn't you come see me sooner? Why now? What's changed?"

---

47. Truman G. Madsen, "Joseph Smith Lecture 1: The First Vision and Its Aftermath" (Brigham Young University devotional, Aug. 22, 1978), 6, speeches.byu.edu.

Andrew shared that he initially felt ashamed for falling short of living the things he'd known to be true. He worried about the consequences that confessing to his bishop might bring. He worried that his family or others would find out what he'd done.

"I rationalized that I didn't need to confess," Andrew said. "I told myself that I could take care of it myself. But every time I took the sacrament, or read the scriptures, or listened to a talk in church or general conference, all I could feel was guilt for what I'd done. I continually felt I was hiding something."

As Andrew tried to cover his sins and ignore the promptings of the Holy Ghost, the gospel brought only a remembrance of his sins instead of peace. That guilt gradually changed to anger and bitterness.

"After a while," he said, "I started to tell myself that the Church was the problem. That the standards of the gospel were too high. That the prophets and apostles were wrong. That it was everyone else's fault for making me feel guilty and not mine."

Andrew began to think about leaving the Church. He thought about where he could go or move where he could stop attending church without his family knowing. What began with unresolved sin and delayed repentance devolved into doubt.

In this chapter, we're going to talk about the relationship between repentance and doubt. We'll discuss how repentance is an essential step in our process of obtaining, developing, and maintaining a witness of truth through the Holy Ghost. I'll also share how Andrew's story ends.

The Body's Response to Physical Trauma

Before we talk about how repentance relates to doubt, let me share a personal experience that may provide an interesting analogy.

Some of you may have experienced firsthand how the human body responds to severe physical trauma, such as a broken bone or other major injury. When we experience a physical injury, certain parts of our brain and nervous system kick in to protect us. One of the most important and essential functions of those systems is to produce the sensation of pain. Pain is meant to signal to us that something is wrong and needs immediate attention. Pain is also intended to protect us from further injury.

I had the experience of breaking my collarbone right near the end of a fantastic mountain bike ride. After performing some aerial acrobatics over the handlebars and attempting to tuck and roll as I hit the ground, I thought I'd landed safely. But as I attempted to get up and brush myself off, my body let me know that something was very, very wrong. Every attempt to move was met with a mounting, excruciating pain in my left shoulder. At one point, I tried to push through it to stand, after which I quickly became lightheaded and had to lie back down. In that moment, my brain was sending two important messages: (1) don't move and (2) you need to get help. My body actually threatened to lose consciousness, if needed, to keep me immobile so as to prevent further injury.

Now, after a little while, another physiological response kicks in. Our central nervous system begins to produce endorphins. Endorphins are essentially the body's natural pain medication, a natural morphine-like substance. Endorphins also help give us a sense of well-being or optimism, making it possible to think and act constructively in a moment of high stress, such as injury. This natural painkiller can numb the pain of trauma enough to enable us to function so that we can do what's needed to get us to safety and address the injury. This endorphin response is temporary, however, and eventually we're left again with the pain to remind us that our injury needs to be taken care of.

Within about twenty minutes after breaking my collarbone, my endorphins provided enough relief so that I could make my way off the trail, to my car, and to the hospital emergency room.

Our Spirit's Response to Trauma

Like our bodies, our spirits are equipped with built-in mechanisms to protect us when we encounter spiritual trauma. Our spirits are of divine origin. In our premortal life, we lived in the presence of our Heavenly Father, immersed in light and truth. Light and truth are part of who we are (see Doctrine and Covenants 93:29). Given our spiritual upbringing, our spirits inherently know when we experience a spiritual injury or trauma. That trauma can occur when we exercise our agency to act in ways contrary to our divine nature, or as a result of the harmful actions of others.

When we commit sin or act contrary to light and truth, we promptly begin to experience one of our spirit's protective mechanisms: guilt. Just as our bodies produce pain in response to physical injury, our spirits experience guilt in response to spiritual injury. Those feelings of guilt are meant to let us know that something is very, very wrong and that our spirit needs help. Guilt, like physical pain, is meant to immobilize us and direct all our energy toward getting the help we need to fix the problem.

Shortly after a spiritual injury occurs, another mechanism kicks in: the voice of the Holy Ghost that brings us hope. Like the endorphins our bodies produce in response to physical injury, the Holy Ghost gives us the strength and direction to get back to spiritual safety and address the spiritual injury we've incurred. The Holy Ghost will prompt us to "look unto [Christ] in every thought" (Doctrine and Covenants 6:36) and to His servants. Those promptings from the Spirit will encourage us to repent, to acknowledge our mistake, to recognize we've acted contrary to our divine nature, to confess our sins, and to make changes. If the sin is serious enough, we will be prompted by the Spirit to talk with our bishop or stake president.

This is where my friend Andrew found himself. His actions led him to cause a spiritual injury to himself and others, and he experienced the accompanying feelings of guilt. Right from the beginning, the Holy Ghost had been prompting him to seek help and repent.

Choosing between Repentance and Doubt

Two days after breaking my collarbone, I sat in front of an extremely competent orthopedic surgeon. The ER x-rays confirmed that my collarbone had been shattered very uncleanly into three separate pieces, and I had a decision to make.

"You can let it heal on its own," the surgeon explained. "Your body will eventually figure out how to deal with what's there. It's likely that the bone fragments won't fuse together. It will take longer and you'll likely have some lasting deformity and lack of strength on that side. It could also lead to other issues like back problems."

The alternative was surgery. "We go in and attach a titanium plate and screws to hold all the bone fragments together so they can heal," the surgeon explained. "The healing time is much faster, and you should be able to return to normal activity. We can do the surgery tomorrow morning if you want."

The surgery obviously had costs and consequences associated with it. There are risks inherent with any surgical procedure. I'd be under anesthesia for several hours. I'd need to wear a sling for several weeks and abandon all my usual fitness activities for a time before gradually returning to normal activity. I'd carry a long scar across my shoulder. There would be a numb feeling near the surgical site that would gradually diminish over time but perhaps never go away entirely. I fretted over what my health insurance would and wouldn't cover.

So . . . what would you do? Would you choose the surgery, or would you let things progress on their own and see how it turns out? One thing was certain: the pain I was experiencing every time I unwisely moved was a constant reminder that this needed attention.

Similarly, when we incur a spiritual injury through sin, we have a choice to make. We can choose to yield to the promptings of the Holy Ghost to seek the help of the Master Physician, Jesus Christ, to address and resolve the problem through the repentance process. Or we can choose to suppress the feelings of guilt and the whisperings of the Holy Ghost and let the injury progress on its own. The latter choice can have devastating consequences.

What we cannot choose is to ignore the problem without consequence. That option doesn't exist. Just as the physical pain I experienced from my fractured collarbone was relentlessly reminding me I needed help, the guilt we experience as a result of sin will not go away on its own. That guilt is an unbearable and constant reminder that we have acted contrary to our divine nature and that we need to fix the problem.

If our fears lead us to avoid the repentance process, our spirits will search for other ways to numb the feelings of guilt and block out the voice of the Holy Ghost. And doubt is one of the most common numbing agents the adversary points us to for a false sense of comfort when we avoid repentance. But using doubt to cover the pain of sin is the spiritual equivalent of perpetually using narcotics to cover the pain of a physical injury and avoiding medical attention. The injury is still there; we're just trying to convince ourselves it's not a problem.

This is the wrestle Andrew experienced. The Spirit was prompting him to trust in the Savior, put off his fears of what others might think, go see his bishop for help, confess his sins, and be willing to do whatever was necessary to get things fixed. After a while, the only alternative was to attempt to numb or cover up the pain of his injured spirit. So he began to rationalize his sins. Andrew tried to convince himself that the Spirit's promptings were wrong, that the Church was the real problem, that the standards of chastity the Lord has established were unrealistic, and that he wasn't to blame for his sins or his feelings of guilt.

Avoiding repentance will eventually result in a loss of our testimony because we're forced to reject truth and the promptings of the Holy Ghost in order to rationalize our decision not to acknowledge or repent of our sins. Here is how the process is described in scripture: "When we undertake to cover our sins, . . . behold, the heavens withdraw themselves; the Spirit of the Lord is grieved; and when it is withdrawn, Amen to the priesthood or the authority of that man. Behold, ere he is aware, he is left unto himself, to kick against the pricks, to persecute the saints, and to fight against God" (Doctrine and Covenants 121:37–38).

As we delay repentance, we must continue to ignore the Holy Ghost's promptings. The Lord has said, "My spirit will not always strive with man" (Ether 2:15). Over time we ignore the Spirit enough that we become numb and a spiritual darkening of the mind occurs. Our ability to discern truth from error by the voice of the Spirit becomes compromised. Because we refuse to hear the Spirit's voice regarding the thing that most needs our attention—our repentance—the Spirit withdraws and we are left to our own intellect to answer the questions that matter most.

A Better Way: The Lord's Way

When we come face to face with the reality of our sins and imperfections, we don't have to choose fear and doubt. We can instead look to our Savior for help and healing. The Savior's gift of repentance through His Atonement is the only balm that will heal the spiritual trauma of our sins and bring the peace we're seeking.

In the second principle, we talked about how merciful the Lord is toward us. The Savior has said, "I came not to judge the world, but to save the world" (John 12:47).

As we discussed when we studied the principle of remembering God's mercy, too many of us have mistakenly set the bar far too high for ourselves, believing that anything less than a flawless performance in this life is a reflection of our value and worth. Such a mistaken perspective makes failure look like an irredeemable act. In fact, such a perspective originates with Satan, and it denies the gospel and power of Jesus Christ and His Atonement.

Perfection was never an expectation for us in this life. Learning to put off the natural man and subdue our physical bodies is expected to be an experience of repeated learning, making mistakes, failing, repenting, and gradually improving and changing. Our Savior willingly suffered for our sins specifically so we could have that opportunity.

Elder Lynn G. Robbins of the Presidency of the Seventy explained it beautifully when he taught, "Repentance is God's ever-accessible gift that allows and enables us to go from failure to failure without any loss of enthusiasm. Repentance isn't His backup plan in the event we might fail. Repentance *is* His plan, knowing that we will."[48]

My dear friend, if you have found yourself caught in this moment of decision—having to choose between repenting of sins or giving into doubt and leaving the Church to numb the pain of guilt you've experienced—I plead with you to consider again this plea from the Savior: "Behold, mine arm of mercy is extended towards you, and whosoever will come, him will I receive; and blessed are those who come unto me. . . . Therefore repent, and come unto me ye ends of the earth, and be saved" (3 Nephi 9:14, 22).

I give my sure personal witness and knowledge that the Lord is merciful. He is not punitive. He has only one interest, and that is to save us. And saving us means changing us into creatures filled with glory and light, capable of receiving a fulness of joy, capable of living an eternal life of happiness. And He can't change us until we submit, which means humbling ourselves, swallowing our pride, admitting we're wrong, and asking for His help.

---

48. Lynn G. Robbins, "Until Seventy Times Seven," *Ensign*, May 2018, 22.

The Blessing of Confession

One of the steps many Church members get stuck on when needing to access the Lord's gift of repentance is the need to confess serious sins to priesthood leaders. The fear of confessing can be one of the primary motivations to avoid the repentance process. And yet the Lord has indicated that confession is essential to repentance. He has said, "Behold, he who has repented of his sins, the same is forgiven, and I, the Lord, remember them no more. By this ye may know if a man repenteth of his sins—behold, he will confess them and forsake them" (Doctrine and Covenants 58:42–43).

And again, "Verily I say unto you, I, the Lord, forgive sins unto those who confess their sins before me and ask forgiveness" (Doctrine and Covenants 64:7). And the Apostle John wrote, "If we confess our sins, he is faithful and just to forgive us our sins, and to cleanse us from all unrighteousness" (1 John 1:9).

I've already spoken about what a difficult and courageous step it is to go see our priesthood leaders for help, especially when that help involves confessing our sins and mistakes. Now may I suggest a few reasons why I believe the Lord has made confession an essential part of the repentance process?

First, confession brings our problem out of darkness and into the light. As I mentioned previously, when we seek to cover our sins, Satan effectively keeps us in his corner of the boxing ring where he's got exclusive opportunity to work on our minds and hearts. As soon as we include one of the Lord's ordained representatives in our struggle, Satan and his lies are exposed and his power over us weakens. When we confess, we no longer have to bear the burden of sin alone. We now have an ally in our priesthood leader who's been ordained and prepared to help us work through the problem.

Second, confession is an act of humility and submission to our Savior. When we work up the courage to confess our sins to our priesthood leader, we are signaling to Christ that we are humble enough to put His will above our fears. We demonstrate that what matters most to us is our relationship with Him, and we prioritize that over any potential embarrassment or other earthly consequence we might incur. I believe the Lord requires this level of humility as we come unto Him.

I think it is this humility the Lord speaks of when he says, "And ye shall offer for a sacrifice unto me a broken heart and a contrite spirit. . . . Therefore, whoso repenteth and cometh unto me as a little child, him will I receive, for of such is the kingdom of God" (3 Nephi 9:20, 22).

One of the responsibilities of bishops and stake presidents is to act as a "judge in Israel" (Doctrine and Covenants 107:72). It is my experience that the judgment these priesthood leaders are given is not to condemn. Rather, they are given judgment and discernment to know how to save. They become an extension of the Savior in helping us to come unto Christ. They become facilitators in the process of repentance.

If the Spirit has been prompting you to seek the help of your bishop or stake president to help you resolve sin, and your fears are keeping you from taking that important step, perhaps the example of one of my heroes, one of the Lord's anointed Apostles, will give you some courage.

President Henry B. Eyring, while at the time serving as president of Ricks College in Rexburg, Idaho, recorded this experience in his journal on June 15, 1975:

> My lesson this morning in the Young Adults class was on Gethsemane. As I sat in the class before teaching, I felt an impression to teach that Christ's sacrifice should lead us to be willing to sacrifice for Him and for salvation of our brothers and sisters. That conviction motivated me through home teaching and genealogy with the boys and, even more, during a temple recommend interview with Bishop Forsgren and President Peterson. I felt impressed to make a serious attempt to confess every unresolved sin, to show my appreciation for the Atonement by taking all the steps necessary for it to work in my life. Bishop Forsgren said, "Now, I urge you to seek direct confirmation of forgiveness from the Lord." And President Peterson said, "This will be one of the most important days in your life."[49]

---

49. Robert I. Eaton and Henry J. Eyring, *I Will Lead You Along: The Life of Henry B. Eyring* (Salt Lake City, UT: Deseret Book, 2013), Deseret Bookshelf.

Now, I don't expect we should suppose President Eyring of any grievous sin. But I'm grateful for his example in showing that all of us—no matter what callings we've held in the Church, no matter how well we've striven to live the commandments—will at some point in our lives, or even at multiple points in our lives, find ourselves in this moment of desiring more than anything to come unto Christ and be sanctified by His Atonement. And in that moment, each of us will recognize that confessing our sins to one of His chosen representatives is an essential part of that process.

The Peace of Repentance

So what about Andrew? "One day," Andrew said, "as I was wrestling with guilt and blaming the Church for making me feel guilty, I heard a voice in my mind that essentially said, 'This isn't anyone's fault but yours. It was your actions that led you to this, not the Church, your leaders, or anyone else.'" Maybe that sounds like a tough message, but it was evidently what Andrew needed to hear. With that message, Andrew also received renewed feelings of hope from the Holy Ghost and promptings to repent. Andrew once again opened his heart to the feelings of godly sorrow that allowed him to muster the courage to visit his bishop.

As for my broken collarbone, the right decision was to acknowledge the extent of my injury and be willing to accept the help of a trained surgeon to address the problem. I chose surgery, and after a few months of pain and inconvenience, I was back to mountain biking and all my other favorite physical activities. I bear a scar on my shoulder as a reminder. And the titanium plate inside my shoulder, placed there by a skilled physician, serves as built-in speedometer, reminding me now to ride my age.

Most of us are familiar with the significant conversion experience of Alma the Younger that we find in the Book of Mormon. Regarding his repentance process with the Lord, Alma stated, "The Lord in mercy hath seen fit to snatch me out of an everlasting burning, and I am born of God. My soul hath been redeemed from the gall of bitterness and bonds of iniquity. I was in the darkest abyss; but now I behold the marvelous light of God. My soul was racked with eternal torment; but I am snatched, and my soul is pained no more" (Mosiah 27:28–29).

The peace Alma experienced and the resulting, life-changing relationship with our Redeemer, Jesus Christ, is available to each of us as we put off the temptation to doubt and instead embrace the Savior's loving gift of repentance. That step of repentance is an essential element in our ability to hear the voice of the Holy Ghost as we seek answers to our sincere questions.

The Spiritual Trauma of Abuse

Before we conclude this principle, we should pause for a moment to briefly discuss a very difficult but related subject. There are other ways our spirits can experience spiritual trauma beyond the actions of our own sins. One of the most harmful forms of spiritual trauma is that which is brought on by physical, emotional, or sexual abuse.

Victims of abuse may experience feelings of guilt similar to those brought on by sin but in a far more complex way. When we commit sin, we are able to correlate those feelings back to our own actions. Victims of abuse, however, do not have this benefit. The sinner has repentance at their disposal to overcome guilt, but the victim of abuse cannot find peace in repentance because they have not committed sin. Abuse victims therefore often grapple with guilt and shame but don't know how to escape it.

Often the victim's mind searches for some explanation as to why this terrible, heinous act has happened to them. It is not uncommon for victims of abuse to convince themselves that if this pain and guilt was not a result of their own actions, it must then be a reflection of who they are as a person. Victims may come to believe they suffered this abuse because they somehow deserved it, because they are inherently unworthy, because they are somehow being punished for who they were in the premortal existence, because they don't fit into God's kingdom, or because God does not love them. This can lead to a lifetime of confusion, self-doubt, inability to feel and express love, difficulty in feeling God's love, or inability to accept Christ's Atonement in their lives.

Similar to the adversary's tactic when we commit sin, he will do everything in his power to convince the victim to hide the abuse, to hide their pain and shame, and to not seek help. The adversary does this to keep them trapped. The effects of the spiritual trauma of abuse will often manifest themselves later in life as anxiety, depression, broken relationships, or inexplicable but persistent physical health problems.

The problem can be further compounded as the victim may begin to act in ways that match this incorrect self-image of themselves, which can lead to sin, thus compounding the guilt they experience. The feelings of guilt and shame that accompany the trauma of abuse can similarly lead to doubt and an inability to feel comfortable in the Lord's Church. The effects of abuse are amplified when suffered at the hands of family members, Church members, or Church leaders who were expected to provide a protective and safe environment.

It is imperative that we state clearly and without confusion that those who have suffered abuse are not guilty of sin. However, victims of abuse absolutely do need the help of the Savior and His Atonement to heal from their spiritual trauma. They will need the help of ordained, understanding, informed, righteous priesthood leaders to help them through that process. And they will nearly always require the help of trained professional counselors who know how to safely guide the victim to recover from the trauma and correct incorrect thinking. It is particularly helpful when those professionals know how to involve Christ's Atonement in the healing process.

If you have been a victim of such hurtful acts—and the voice of the adversary has been trying to convince you, perhaps over the course of your entire life, that you are unworthy or that God does not love you—you need to know that these are lies. The pain you have suffered is a result of the hurtful actions of others and not a reflection of your worth and value as a son or daughter of God. Your Heavenly Father and your Savior love you, and they grieve tremendously at what you have experienced. And while it may seem impossible to you now, the Savior does have the ability to heal your wounds and make you whole again. He loves you more than you can know, and He stands ready and eager to help you. Some of the resources listed in the "Exercises" section at the end of this chapter may help you get started.

Act in Faith: Embrace the Savior's Gift of Repentance

In this principle, we've studied how avoiding repentance can lead to doubt. How can we apply this in our search for a witness of the truthfulness of the gospel and answers to our sincere questions? I expect that all of us have some burden of sin, great or small, that the Spirit has been prompting us to unload. Sometimes these sins are minor and may only require that we acknowledge them with the Lord, seek His forgiveness, and ask for His help to change. And some cannot be resolved without the help of a priesthood leader.

As you consider your wrestle with doubt, is unresolved sin possibly limiting you from receiving a witness from the Holy Ghost of the truths of the restored gospel? Have you found yourself seeking to rationalize mistakes or find fault in the Church or Church members to avoid the pain of guilt that accompanies unresolved sin? Are there moments when you've felt the Holy Ghost prompting you to take care of this, but you've avoided those promptings out of fear? If this is part of what you're experiencing, what actions can you take now to look to the Savior and replace that doubt and fear with the peace of Christ's infinite Atonement through the gift of repentance?

To act in faith on this principle, I invite each of us to find a quiet space and reach out to our Heavenly Father in sincere prayer and consider asking these two questions: (1) "Father, are there any unresolved sins that I need to take care of?" and (2) "If so, what do you want me to do?"

Listen for the feelings and thoughts that come. Then this time, instead of avoiding those promptings like you may have done before, act on them. And if the Spirit prompts you to reach out to your bishop or stake president, you can do so knowing that the Lord is with you as you move forward in faith.

I give my personal witness of Christ's infinite mercy and loving nature. I know firsthand His ability to heal the wounds of sin in our lives. And I know the great blessing of priesthood leaders who the Lord ordains and inspires to guide us through that process. A deeper, more personal relationship with our Savior Jesus Christ awaits each of us as we accept His invitation to "come unto [Him] . . . and be saved" (3 Nephi 9:22).

Exercises

Ponder the following questions and write down your thoughts.

- As you consider your identified doubts and sincere questions, are there any that may have originated with your own shortcomings or sins?
- What promptings did you get as you acted in faith to ask the Lord what unresolved sins you may have in your life? Did the Spirit prompt you to take any actions? What are they? Write them down. How will you go about acting on them? When will you act on them?
- Study the scriptures referenced in the Topical Guide under the topic "Confession." Why do you believe the Lord has made confession an essential part of the repentance process? What past experiences have you had as you've sincerely confessed your sins?
- If needed, please refer to the following resources for leaders, family members, and victims regarding abuse:
    - The Church's website for resources relating to abuse: abuse.ChurchofJesusChrist.org.
    - Ann F. Pritt, "Healing the Spiritual Wounds of Sexual Abuse," *Ensign*, Apr. 2001, 58–63.
    - Priesthood leaders should also be familiar with and follow the guidelines given by the Church for responding to and reporting abuse, currently found on the following web page: https://www.churchofjesuschrist.org/get-help/abuse/protecting-members-and-reporting-abuse.

Principle 9: Keep the Commandments

"Thus if you have really handed yourself over to [Christ], it must follow that you are trying to obey Him. But trying in a new way, a less worried way. Not doing these things in order to be saved, but because He has begun to save you already. Not hoping to get to Heaven as a reward for your actions, but inevitably wanting to act in a certain way because a first faint gleam of Heaven is already inside you." (C. S. Lewis)[50]

One of the most impressive choices Amy made during her wrestle with doubt was to continue to live the gospel and keep the commandments and her covenants. Despite the doubts Amy was experiencing about the Church, which were leading her to question the very foundations of her faith, Amy chose to continue to live the principles and truths she'd been taught and received a witness of throughout her life. I believe Amy's demonstration of faith was critical in her receiving a renewed witness of the restored gospel.

For most Latter-day Saints, a large part of our testimony has come gradually over time, little by little, through the daily small and simple acts of living the gospel. You have already exercised great faith in your life as you've followed Christ into the waters of baptism,

---

50. C. S. Lewis, *Mere Christianity* (New York: Simon & Schuster Touchstone, 1996), 131.

made sacred covenants, attended church, partaken regularly of the sacrament, served in church callings, studied the scriptures, offered prayers, attended seminary, participated in youth activities, listened to the words of living prophets and apostles, participated in temple ordinances, lived the Word of Wisdom, or paid an honest tithe. Through your daily acts of faith and looking to Christ, you've been able to gain invaluable personal experience regarding the great peace and blessings that are available when you strive to live a godlike life. Your faithful living of the gospel has also afforded you many opportunities for the Holy Ghost to bear witness to your heart of the goodness and truthfulness of the Lord's restored gospel. That personal experience is a powerful witness of truth.

So what do we do when we're faced with new thoughts, feelings, and information that cause us to question that testimony of experience we've developed? Elder Neil L. Andersen taught, "How do you remain 'steadfast and immovable' during a trial of faith? You immerse yourself in the very things that helped build your core of faith: you exercise faith in Christ, you pray, you ponder the scriptures, you repent, you keep the commandments, and you serve others."[51]

When the foundations of our faith are being tested, one of the most empowering principles we can embrace is to choose to continue to live the gospel and keep the commandments while we patiently seek for answers to our sincere questions.

A Witness of the Gospel Comes as We Live It

The Savior taught that a witness of the gospel comes to those who are willing, first, to live it. "My doctrine is not mine, but his that sent me," He taught. "If any man will do his will, he shall know of the doctrine, whether it be of God, or whether I speak of myself" (John 7:16–17).

In this dispensation the Lord also explained the necessity of living the commandments to obtain a knowledge of truth, saying, "He that keepeth [the] commandments receiveth truth and light, until he is glorified in truth and knoweth all things" (Doctrine and Covenants 93:28).

---

51. Neil L. Andersen, "Trial of Your Faith," *Ensign*, Nov. 2012, 40.

Simply put, a testimony that the commandments, principles, doctrines, and teachings of the restored gospel are true comes as we live them. The Holy Ghost will give us enough prompting and motivation to help us start, but as Christ indicated, if we want to "know the doctrine, whether it be of God" (John 7:17), we need to be willing to demonstrate our faith by choosing to live it.

I previously shared the experience of the wonderful sister who struggled mightily to develop enough faith to live the law of tithing. That good sister had not yet received a testimony of tithing because she had not yet experienced the blessings of living it. Once she mustered the faith to act, first by asking the Lord sincere questions and then by choosing to live the law of tithing, He was able to give her a witness through personal experience that the law was true and that He would bless her for living it. As the prophet Moroni wrote, "Dispute not because ye see not, for ye receive no witness until after the trial of your faith" (Ether 12:6).

If we wish to "see" whether the gospel is true, we must first "try" our faith. When doubt threatens to consume us, we can signal to our Heavenly Father and our Savior our sincere desire to know and do their will by deliberately choosing to live the gospel and keep their commandments. Living the gospel is one way we "look unto [Christ] in every thought" (Doctrine and Covenants 6:36) when doubts arise.

Obedience Qualifies Us for the Holy Ghost

Obedience to the commandments qualifies us for the companionship of the Holy Ghost. You're probably familiar with the Savior's words to His disciples when He stated He would send them the Holy Ghost to guide and comfort them. But when we look closely, we notice there is a very important verse preceding that promise. Christ said, "If ye love me, keep my commandments. And I will pray the Father, and he shall give you another Comforter, that he may abide with you for ever; Even the Spirit of truth; whom the world cannot receive, because it seeth him not, neither knoweth him: but ye know him; for he dwelleth with you, and shall be in you" (John 14:15–17).

Note the Savior's indication to His disciples that keeping His commandments was an essential precursor that would enable Him to send them the Spirit of truth. Elder Robert D. Hales taught, "Living the commandments brings us into harmony with Deity; we become one in purpose with the Father and the Son. When we are one with God, we walk with spiritual light. Our diligence in keeping the commandments allows the Holy Ghost to dwell within us. We are given the gift of personal revelation. This is a spiritual light that protects us and serves as a beacon, guiding us in righteous ways. It dispels the darkness of the adversary."[52]

The spiritual light and gift of revelation that Elder Hales spoke of are something we desperately need when we're wrestling with doubt and seeking answers to the questions of the soul. We can lay claim on those promised blessings as we exercise our agency to live the commandments even as we pass through a trial of faith.

The Adversary Will Attempt to Separate Us from Living the Gospel

When our faith and testimony are being tried, the adversary sees great opportunity to separate us from Christ and the Holy Ghost. One of the deceptive tactics Satan uses is to persuade us that our doubts give us justification to step away from living the principles and commandments we once knew to be true. His persuasive argument is that it's fair and reasonable for us to experiment with abandoning our covenants.

Satan's arguments essentially go something like this: "You know, since you're having doubts, why not try *not* living the gospel for a while? Then you'll get a good sense of whether it's right for you or not. So why not skip church for a while? You've been passing up coffee and alcohol all your life; since you're not sure how you feel about the Word of Wisdom, why not go have some fun with that for once? You're not sure how you feel about the temple, so why not stop wearing your temple garments? That oppressive law of chastity is way too hard to measure up to anyway, so why not relax with that and enjoy yourself? And why are you still paying you're tithing?"

Do these voices sound at all familiar? It's a brilliant tactic. If Satan can separate us from doing the things that contributed to our

---

52. Robert D. Hales, "If Thou Wilt Enter into Life, Keep the Commandments," *Ensign*, May 1996, 36.

testimony in the first place, perhaps he can keep us there long enough that we begin to forget or can't feel the Holy Ghost anymore, or far worse . . . until we no longer want to. Recall again the words of Nephi when he taught that Satan "leadeth them by the neck with a flaxen cord, until he bindeth them with his strong cords forever" (2 Nephi 26:22).

But the adversary's reasoning is completely contrary to Christ's counsel and teachings. When we reduce our involvement in living the gospel, we reduce opportunity for the Holy Ghost to bear witness of the truth. If we actively decide to abandon sacred covenants or commit serious sin as a response to our doubts, we look away from Christ and severely compromise our ability to hear the voice of the Holy Ghost at the very moment when we most need His guidance.

Indeed, one of the worst things we can do during a trial of our faith is to abandon our covenants and justify committing sin. It's kind of like throwing all the fire extinguishers out of the house after a fire starts, then diving headlong into the flames so we can experience just how hot they really are.

If we have been experiencing this—voices that are trying to convince us that abandoning living the gospel is the right way through a trial of faith—we need to look unto Christ, counsel with our priesthood leaders, and ask our Heavenly Father in prayer to help us recognize where those voices are coming from. If they are prompting us to do things which are contrary to the commandments of God, which would lead us away into temptation and sin, or which separate us from the Holy Ghost, we can know that those voices are not seeking to help us but to hurt us. Those voices may come from within ourselves or from the adversary or his followers, but they do not come from the Lord. Our Heavenly Father will never prompt us to do something that would lead us further away from Him.

Beware the Alma Experience

A beloved account from the Book of Mormon is the incredible conversion experience of Alma the Younger. The account is found largely in Mosiah 27 and recounted again by Alma to his son Helaman in Alma 36. We learn that Alma had become "a very wicked and an idolatrous man. And he was a man of many words, and did speak much flattery to the people; therefore he led many of the people to do after the manner of his iniquities" (Mosiah 27:8). Alma also tells us that he "went about with the sons of Mosiah, seeking to destroy the Church of God" (Alma 36:6). And Mormon comments that they were "the very vilest of sinners" (Mosiah 28:4).

We all know the story. One day, as these friends were going about seeking to destroy the faith of Church members, an angel appeared to them. With great power, the angel severely chastised them for their actions. The angel said to Alma, "If thou wilt of thyself be destroyed, seek no more to destroy the Church of God" (Alma 36:9). In other words, "Alma, if you want to be destroyed yourself, go ahead—but all this trying to take others with you ends now."

This heavenly encounter was enough to shake Alma to a recognition of his sins and the realization that he could lose his soul. Alma fell to the ground and for the space of two days was unconscious, unable to move or speak. During this time, Alma experienced a dramatic conversion to Christ. When he finally awakened, he explained, "I have repented of my sins, and have been redeemed of the Lord; behold I am born of the Spirit" (Mosiah 27:24).

Alma subsequently went on to lead the Church and bring many, many souls to Christ. It's a beautiful, miraculous, and true account of a man who was rescued and redeemed through the mercy and Atonement of Christ through sincere, humble repentance.

Occasionally, I will encounter Church members who seem to be seeking an Alma experience. Sometimes we try to seek a witness of the truth in a reverse approach by intentionally rebelling against the Church and God's commandments, almost as some sort of test. In such cases, we may develop a mentality that goes something like, "Well, if I'm wrong, then the Lord will eventually stop me." Those with children are familiar with this behavior. It's a common experience for a child to intentionally disobey, all the while making sure the parent is watching, looking for the expected reaction of correction or frustration from the parent. The child tests to ensure the parent is still there and cares enough about their well-being to step in when needed. It's a plea for attention.

But I'm not sure we can or should expect the Lord to provide us with a witness of truth through this approach. Let me explain why I think this method of seeking a witness of truth is neither effective nor something we should want to try.

Let's first consider what Alma went through. He described his experience using words such as this: "I was racked with eternal torment. . . . I was tormented with the pains of hell. . . . The very thought of coming into the presence of my God did rack my soul with inexpressible horror. . . . I was racked, even with the pains of a damned soul" (Alma 36:12–14, 16).

That is about the strongest language I think anyone could use to describe what it feels like to be truly cut off from the presence of God. Whatever Alma experienced is something I believe very few individuals can understand and something none of us, if we understood it, would ever intentionally seek.

Alma also stated that his conversion included "repenting nigh unto death" (Mosiah 27:28). It's worth considering that Alma might not have successfully made it through this experience had conditions been slightly different. In fact, I would suggest that perhaps most of us would not physically or spiritually survive such an experience. After all, the Book of Mormon also contains the accounts of Sherem, Nehor, and Korihor, all of whom were likewise on a rebellious path of destruction, all of whom were testing God and asking His prophets to prove to them the error of their ways so they could believe. None of these men's fates was as fortunate as Alma's.

Sherem also fell to the earth and was harrowed up by his sins for many days. But Sherem's fate was quite different than Alma's. Before Sherem died, he stated, "I fear lest I have committed the unpardonable sin, for I have lied unto God. . . . I greatly fear lest my case shall be awful; but I confess unto God" (Jacob 7:19).

Alma was the exception to the rule, not the norm. If we choose to seek the Alma experience, we're really choosing the Sherem, Nehor, and Korihor experience but hoping we're somehow an exception.

And finally, the problem with this reversed approach to seeking a witness of truth is that God is already constantly reaching out to us trying to show us the right path. He's sent prophets and apostles to teach and warn us. He works miracles in our lives every day. He continuously sends the still, small voice of the Holy Ghost to whisper to us which way we should go. Seeking a witness of truth by rebelling against it means we have to reject all the efforts God is already making with us.

If we've decided to attempt this path of intentional disobedience to the commandments—knowingly exercising our agency contrary to the witnesses of truth we've already received in hopes that God will miraculously intervene to stop us—we should remember these words from the Savior: "My Spirit will not always strive with man; wherefore, if ye will sin until ye are fully ripe ye shall be cut off from the presence of the Lord" (Ether 2:15).

Now, there is a part of the Alma experience we should all seek and that the Lord wants us to seek. Alma explained it this way: "All mankind, yea, men and women, all nations, kindreds, tongues and people, must be born again; yea, born of God, changed from their carnal and fallen state, to a state of righteousness, being redeemed of God, becoming his sons and daughters; And thus they become new creatures; and unless they do this, they can in nowise inherit the kingdom of God" (Mosiah 27:25–26). That conversion is something each of us should absolutely seek. But none of us need to go down the path of rebellion to experience that mighty change of heart.

I believe that if we could have the great blessing of having a one-on-one interview with Alma, he would seek to warn us—with all the same words and energy of soul that he used with his son Helaman—*not* to go down the path he walked. I think he would emphatically plead with us, "Don't do what I did! You have no idea what it's like. It's not worth it. You most likely won't make it back. Listen to the witnesses of truth that God is already giving you."

What made the difference for Alma was not the magnitude of the heavenly visitation he received. What made the difference for Alma was this decision: "I cried within my heart: O Jesus, thou Son of God, have mercy on me" (Alma 36:18).

That is a decision each of us can make today. We don't need to get God's attention—we already have it. We don't need to walk away from the teachings of the gospel to gain a witness of them. We don't need to leave the Lord's Church to discover it's true. We can instead remember, once again, Christ's loving, heartfelt plea when He states, "Draw near unto me and I will draw near unto you; seek me diligently and ye shall find me; ask, and ye shall receive; knock, and it shall be opened unto you" (Doctrine and Covenants 88:63).

Needing Space?

At one point, my friend Amy chose not to attend church a few Sundays but still ensured that her husband and children attended. On those few Sundays when she did not attend church, she chose to immerse herself in sincere scripture study and prayer, seeking answers to her questions. After spending a few Sundays seeking guidance, she felt the Holy Ghost prompting her that she needed to return to church. She could feel and recognize that something important was missing, and she really wanted to partake of the sacrament again and renew her covenants. The experience ultimately helped strengthen her testimony. "I needed that space to evaluate things on my own," she explained.

Some faithful Church members, as part of their process of overcoming doubt, have felt they needed some space to evaluate how much living the gospel really meant to them. Or perhaps they felt they needed the opportunity to step back and discover or decide if living the gospel was really their choice or something that was imposed on them. Or perhaps they've felt spiritually exhausted trying to keep up with all the requirements they believe that living the gospel demands of them.

I'm not suggesting distancing ourselves from the gospel as a general recommended course of action. As we've just studied, such general advice does not correlate with what Christ has taught us. But I do recognize that some Church members feel this way. One thing that is certainly true is that the decision to live the gospel of Jesus Christ and be part of His restored kingdom on earth must ultimately be a choice that we make for ourselves. And for some individuals, perhaps like the prodigal son, the road to faith evidently ends up including some difficult detours.

If we are experiencing feelings of needing space from the gospel as we work through our questions and doubts, we would be wise to counsel with priesthood leaders and directly with the Lord in prayer as we wisely and intentionally seek inspiration as to whether and why space from the Church is the right thing for us.

Binding the Lord

You'll recall that one of Amy's concerns was that her doubts and fears somehow made her unworthy. Amy's bishop explained that although she was wrestling with doubt, because she was faithfully living the commandments and keeping her covenants, she could go to the Lord with great confidence, knowing that He would be not only *wanting* but also *obligated* to lovingly respond to her prayers and questions. Amy's continued obedience to the commandments enabled her to lay claim on this promise from God: "I, the Lord, am bound when ye do what I say; but when ye do not what I say, ye have no promise" (Doctrine and Covenants 82:10).

As we study the Lord's commandments in the scriptures, we find they are nearly always accompanied with a promise that He is bound by. This is a powerful tool that we can use in our search for truth because we can exercise our faith to keep a commandment knowing that God must provide us the promised blessing associated with that commandment.

Consider the following promises the Lord has made regarding specific commandments. Which of these would be helpful for you personally as you go through your trial of faith and seek answers to your questions?

If you keep the law of the fast, the Lord promises that "thy light [shall] break forth as the morning, . . . thine health shall spring forth speedily, . . . [and] the glory of the Lord shall be thy rearward. . . . Then shalt thou call, and the Lord shall answer; thou shalt cry, and he shall say, Here I am . . . and the Lord shall guide thee continually" (Isaiah 58:8–9, 11).

If you live the law of tithing, the Lord promises that He will "open you the windows of heaven, and pour you out a blessing, that there shall not be room enough to receive it" (Malachi 3:10).

If you keep the Sabbath day holy, the Lord promises us that "the fulness of the earth is yours" (Doctrine and Covenants 59:16).

If you live the Word of Wisdom, the Lord promises you physical health and that you "shall find wisdom and great treasures of knowledge, even hidden treasures" (Doctrine and Covenants 89:19).

As you worthily renew your covenant to remember Christ and keep His commandments through partaking of the sacrament, the Lord promises that "[ye] may always have his Spirit to be with [you]" (Doctrine and Covenants 20:77).

And again, there is the promise from the Savior if you keep His commandments: "I will pray the Father, and he shall give you another Comforter, that he may abide with you for ever; Even the Spirit of truth. . . . I will not leave you comfortless: I will come to you" (John 14:16–18).

When we are in the midst of doubts and worry, desperately seeking answers to the questions of the soul, we so much need to be able to lay claim on those promises from the Savior. We need the comfort of the Holy Ghost. We need Christ to come to us. Each of us can confidently lay claim on those blessings. Each of us can choose to act in faith to keep the Lord's commandments while we search for answers. That is a test the Lord is willing and wanting us to put Him to. If we will use our agency to continue to live the gospel and keep the Lord's commandments in our trial of faith, our Heavenly Father is bound by love and by promise to send us the help we need.

Act in Faith: Use the Commandments in Your Search for Truth

Now it's time to act in faith on this principle. Consider again our list of questions. What blessings has the Lord promised us if we keep His commandments that would help you find the answers you are seeking? Are there specific commandments or principles of the gospel that tie directly or indirectly to your questions? Consider prayerfully seeking guidance from the Lord as you ask, "What commandments or principles can I live that will help me find answers to these questions?"

Exercises

Ponder the following questions and write down your thoughts.

- What is the relationship between keeping the commandments and receiving a witness of the restored gospel?
- Have you been tempted by the adversary to abandon your covenants or the commandments as part of your trial of faith?

How will you choose to respond when those temptations present themselves?

- Often only the Holy Ghost can help us connect the blessings in our lives back to specific commandments or principles that we've chosen to live. As you look back over your life, prayerfully consider what blessings you have received for living specific commandments. Write down the commandment you lived and the blessings you believe you received from living it.
- Consider the Savior's words as found in John 7:16–17. What knowledge have you gained as a result of doing the Lord's will? What gospel principles and commandments do you have a witness of as a result of living them?

Principle 10: Embrace the Gift of Agency

"And the Messiah cometh in the fulness of time, that he may redeem the children of men from the fall. And because that they are redeemed from the fall they have become free forever, knowing good from evil; to act for themselves and not to be acted upon." (2 Nephi 2:26)

Throughout this book we've shared accounts of Church members who've learned to look to Christ by choosing to act on principles of faith. Many of these members have been blessed to develop stronger testimonies of the restored gospel and a closer relationship with their Savior and Heavenly Father.

But we all know that not every member's experience is the same. For every story of restored faith we've shared, we also know of wonderful Church members who haven't yet found the answers they're looking for, or who aren't quite ready to engage in a sincere search for answers, or who are struggling to experience God's mercy for them and others in their lives. We know those who haven't yet found the strength to engage in the healing process of repentance, or who are too hurt from difficult experiences to consider returning to the Lord's Church, or who have decided, at least for the moment, that a life outside the Church is better for them and their family.

While serving as bishop, I was always excited when new members moved into our ward. I'd come to believe that the Lord's hand was always involved in bringing members in and out of our congregation as He worked to accomplish His purposes in our lives. So when I learned that a certain new family had recently moved into our ward, I naturally began to reach out to them. After making a few attempts to visit and leaving some home-baked goodies at their home, they sent me a very kind message thanking me for the ward's outreach but explained that they had made the decision, prior to moving, to no longer participate in the Church. They respectfully requested that they not be included in the ward's efforts to bring them back. They didn't explain their reasons, but I responded that we would, of course, respect their request and that the ward was available for them should they ever need us.

Over the next several months, my thoughts kept coming back to this family, and especially to their children. I just kept feeling like the Lord wanted me to do something to reach out to them, but I wanted to be respectful of their request. I ended up writing a very personal letter to them. I explained that I completely respected their decision and that I really had no desire to pressure them, but I wanted them to know I'd been thinking about them. I shared with them my own experience growing up in an inactive family in the Church and how that impacted my life and teenage years; I felt like I had missed out on many blessings of the gospel for much of my life. I let them know that if they ever felt a desire to return, we'd love and receive them, whatever their concerns might be, and that we could sincerely use their help if they did return. I indicated they didn't need to respond and that we loved and supported them regardless of whether they ever chose to return to church.

Shortly after receiving my letter, the mother of this family asked if we could meet. We arranged a time to visit at the church and had a wonderful conversation. She shared with me her personal journey through the gospel and how her testimony of the restored gospel had eroded over time, beginning with doubts about some of the common topics we've already mentioned, such as the historical practice of plural marriage, concerns about the validity of the Book of Mormon, and so on.

Finally, after sharing all these concerns, she explained that she and her husband believed that one of their children may experience same-sex attraction, and they couldn't see how they could possibly raise their child in the gospel given the Church's teachings regarding chastity and marriage. I wish I could say I had just the right words to say in that meeting to reinvigorate this sister's faith to return to church. But those weren't the words the Spirit gave me that evening. I expressed my love and support for her and her family. We shared several more thoughts that evening, and I asked if she wanted to make an attempt at that time to give the Church and her testimony another try, to which she honestly and kindly responded, "No." I again let her know that we would be here for them in any way they felt we could help.

I was so grateful for this sister's transparency with her faith. Of all the questions that may challenge the faith of Church members in our modern political and social climate, perhaps none has been more recently present and difficult than topics surrounding same-sex attraction and gender identity.

The Church continues to teach and uphold the Lord's celestial standard of marriage between a man and a woman and the standard of abstinence outside of marriage. However, we live in a society where such views have become increasingly unpopular, and Church members who experience same-sex attraction or questions about gender identity face significant, faith-challenging choices. Many family members also wrestle mightily to understand how they can choose to honor their baptismal covenants and sustain the Lord's Church while simultaneously ensuring their family member feels loved, accepted, and supported.

I believe these are challenges that only those who experience them can fully understand or appreciate, with the exception of our Savior, Jesus Christ, who suffered all things so that He would know how to help us in our time of need.

I have not personally passed through these challenges, and I honestly confess that I am unable to speak about this topic through the lens of personal experience. I wholeheartedly believe that none of us is in a position to pass judgment on someone who makes difficult choices about their Church membership as it relates to this topic. And I have personally known and counseled with Church members who have chosen to leave the Church, believing it too difficult to support or live the Church's teachings of chastity and marriage in the face of their own challenges or, more especially, those of a close family member.

But I have also known and studied the accounts of many faithful Latter-day Saints who have chosen to remain true to their covenants and the Lord's law of chastity when they themselves or someone they love experiences same-sex attraction or questions regarding gender identity. In doing so, they've chosen to walk a path far more difficult than most of us can appreciate. These faithful Church members, to me, are modern-day examples of the miraculous faith that Peter demonstrated, figuratively doing the impossible—walking on the water with Christ as their focus and companion, daily relying on Christ's Atonement and sustaining power to get them through the storm.

I believe we can learn so much from these modern-day examples of faith—these people who have confronted the reality that their own natural desires give them legitimate cause to question the validity of the laws and teachings of the Lord's Church and yet choose to stay. Where does this exceeding faith come from? Our personal experiences may not be with same-sex attraction or gender identity, but whatever our trial of faith is, how can we similarly choose to accept the Lord's laws and the teachings of His restored Church when our own desires and unanswered questions would give us reason or excuse to choose a different path?

Aside from the principles we've already discussed, I have learned three important things from these faithful Church members.

First, they have developed a testimony of the fundamental truths of the restored gospel borne out their own personal experiences and through revelation. That testimony enables them to acknowledge their own feelings while simultaneously choosing not to deny what they know to be true. Second, these Church members seem to have truly understood and embraced the Lord's great gift of agency in their lives. And third, they rely daily on the redeeming power of Christ's Atonement for help to exercise their agency to stay faithful to their covenants through their ongoing trial of faith.

Their testimony, coupled with an understanding of agency and a reliance on Christ, has enabled them to make a decision to live the gospel of Jesus Christ even when society around them and their own physical and emotional inclinations give them reason not to.

Similarly for each of us, one of the most empowering moments in our search for truth comes when we understand that our Heavenly Father has structured His plan such that our destiny is in our own hands, and that we ultimately get to choose what it is we want to become. Our agency is fundamental to our existence and of the utmost priority to our Heavenly Father and our Savior, Jesus Christ. Understanding and embracing the agency They've given us is one of the most essential ways we look unto Christ as we seek to overcome doubt and act in faith.

However, our agency can only empower us to the degree we understand the choices we're making. As we mature spiritually, we begin to understand that there is no decision we make that does not produce a corresponding result or consequence. We discover that our agency is accompanied with laws and boundaries to which all beings in the universe are subject, including God.

The plan of our Heavenly Father for His children is designed to provide the maximum possible range of expression of our agency and the maximum opportunity for joy and happiness. When we study God's plan in depth, we discover an intensely sophisticated, perfect system of agency, law, justice, and mercy designed to propel us toward eternal life, while simultaneously allowing us to ultimately decide for ourselves what we will become.

And so, for this final principle, we will seek to understand the glorious truths the Lord has revealed about our agency and how it relates to law, justice, and the great mercy extended to us through the redeeming power of Christ's Atonement. We'll seek to understand why each of these is an essential, inextricable element in God's system of government and His plan to make exaltation and eternal life available to His children. We will also see that our adversary seeks to destroy our agency in every way possible by attacking these principles. We will study how our Heavenly Father has structured His kingdom to provide all of His children a place where they feel most comfortable according to their own desires. The hope is that we, like these examples of faith we've discussed, will walk away better empowered to exercise our agency as we make decisions about our relationship to Christ and His restored Church.

Agency, Law, and Justice

One of the most common sources of doubt can arise when our own desires to make certain choices—to live a certain lifestyle, to fit in socially with others, or even simply to believe what we want to believe—opposes the laws, rules, doctrines, principles, teachings, policies, or practices of the Lord's Church. A natural response in such moments is to question those boundaries, to wonder if they are fair and right or whether they come from the Lord or are man-made, or to ask if we can change the laws and rules to accommodate our desires or make us or our loved ones feel more comfortable.

Corianton, the son of Alma, experienced such doubts and questions. Corianton's wrestle with sin led him to question God's laws regarding chastity (see Alma 39:3). Corianton had the blessing of a father, Alma, who had experienced firsthand the consequences of sin, the boundaries of the laws of God, and the infinite mercy of Christ's Atonement. "And now, my son," said Alma, "I perceive there is somewhat more which doth worry your mind, which ye cannot understand—which is concerning the justice of God" (Alma 42:1).

Faced with the consequences of his own actions in opposition to God's laws, Corianton wondered if it was possible to avoid those consequences altogether, or how it could possibly be fair that he should have to face any consequences at all, or whether the law of chastity was even necessary or legitimate.

If Corianton had gone through our process of converting his doubts into sincere questions, what might some of those questions have been? Let's propose a few sincere questions that Corianton might have asked that might also help us as we study these principles:

- What is the purpose of law?
- Can God change the laws of His kingdom?
- Why doesn't God just alter the law so that everyone can be saved?
- What is the purpose of justice?
- If God is so merciful, why can't He just forgive everyone for their sins and let everyone off the hook? Then nobody would need to suffer the consequences of sin.
- What role does mercy play in the plan of God?
- What is agency and where does it come from?
- Does my agency give me freedom to do whatever I want?

With those sincere questions in mind, let's turn to the words of Christ and His servants in the scriptures to see what the Lord has revealed regarding these eternal principles.

Agency

What is agency? Where does our agency come from? Does our agency have limitations or boundaries, or does agency give us the freedom to choose any outcome we want?

Our Savior revealed the truth about the nature of our agency when He explained, "All truth is independent in that sphere in which God has placed it, to act for itself, as all intelligence also; otherwise there is no existence" (Doctrine and Covenants 93:30).

How's that for an "existential" truth? Existence requires that truth be placed in a sphere where it can act for itself. Agency is the opportunity given to us by God to act for ourselves within the boundaries of the sphere in which we are placed. The greater the sphere in which we can exercise agency, the higher level of existence we can experience. Conversely, a reduced sphere of agency results in a lower potential and level of existence. Thus, our agency—our ability to act—is fundamental to our existence.

Let's consider a simple analogy. Sometime in our teenage years, many of us have the great privilege of obtaining a driver's license. It's a momentous occasion. Suddenly the sphere in which we can exercise our agency gets a lot bigger. We can travel faster and cover greater distances. We can accomplish more in a given amount of time. That driver's license can open doors to new employment and social opportunities. We don't need to wait for parents to provide rides everywhere. This added sphere of agency affords us a new level of independence, a higher level of existence.

Similarly, at some point in our spiritual upbringing, the sphere of our existence—or the boundaries in which we could express our agency—was much smaller than it is today. Recall again this truth revealed by the Savior: "Man was also in the beginning with God. Intelligence, or the light of truth, was not created or made, neither indeed can be" (Doctrine and Covenants 93:29). God, in His goodness, provided an opportunity for us as intelligences to increase our level of existence by expanding the bounds in which we could exercise our agency. How? By providing us the opportunity to become members of His kingdom, and to couple our intelligences with spiritual and physical bodies.

Similar to obtaining a driver's license, gaining a physical body provides a dramatic increase in the space in which we can exercise our agency. Our ability to interact with each other and with matter around us—the range of emotions, sensations, pain, and joy we can experience—have all increased significantly. A physical body opens the door to opportunities not previously available to us. The Lord explained, "For man is spirit. The elements are eternal, and spirit and element, inseparably connected, receive a fulness of joy; And when separated, man cannot receive a fulness of joy. The elements are the tabernacle of God; yea, man is the tabernacle of God" (Doctrine and Covenants 93:33–35).

We also learn that our progression and level of existence is not meant to stop here. Our Heavenly Father intends to increase the sphere in which we can act beyond what we experience today. The Lord told Moses, "For behold, this is my work and my glory—to bring to pass the immortality and eternal life of man" (Moses 1:39).

God's ultimate desire is to provide us the opportunity to live the same level of existence that He lives: eternal life. That godlike life provides the largest possible sphere in which to exercise the full range of our agency. Our Savior has said that those of His children who choose that life "shall have glory added upon their heads for ever and ever" (Abraham 3:26).

However, living that godlike life is not something our Heavenly Father can or desires to force upon us. His plan ultimately allows us to decide how large a sphere of existence, and what range of expression of agency, we desire to have.

The Relationship between Law and Agency

Law is a critical component to agency. Without law, there can be no agency. Law defines the boundaries of the sphere in which we are free to exercise our agency. Returning to our driver's license analogy, when we obtain a driver's license, we learn that the privilege of holding that license is accompanied with a lot of rules and requirements. We take driver's education courses, written exams, and vision tests. We agree to abide by traffic laws and rules of the road as a condition of maintaining the privilege of driving. This elevated level of agency and freedom brings with it an elevated set of laws to which we become subject if we desire to maintain the associated privileges.

Similarly, every increase in the sphere of our agency is accompanied with an associated increase in law. Law defines and establishes the boundaries of our agency.

The Savior taught this eternal truth about law: "All kingdoms have a law given; And there are many kingdoms; for there is no space in the which there is no kingdom; and there is no kingdom in which there is no space, either a greater or a lesser kingdom. And unto every kingdom is given a law; and unto every law there are certain bounds also and conditions. All beings who abide not in those conditions are not justified" (Doctrine and Covenants 88:36–39).

No matter where we go—in every organization on earth or in heaven, in our civic governments, in corporations, in volunteer organizations, in schools, in our social clubs, and even in our friendship circles—we find law. Sometimes that law is formal and written, oftentimes requiring formal agreement to uphold it and live by it. At other times, like in our friendship circles, that law is informal and not spoken of but still present.

The Savior explained that law serves the purpose of protecting, preserving, elevating, or sanctifying those who choose to be governed by it. He said, "And again, verily I say unto you, that which is governed by law is also preserved by law and perfected and sanctified by the same" (Doctrine and Covenants 88:34).

Law establishes the quality of life, the standards of behavior, and the type of environment that members of a society desire to live and maintain. Individuals who agree to abide the law can rightfully expect the protections and quality of life the law provides. The extent to which a society's laws can elevate the lives of its members is dependent on the quality of its laws.

As an example, most societies have laws against theft. Those laws help elevate the quality of life for all citizens by ensuring a measure of peace and confidence that our belongings and assets will not be taken from us. The whole of society and our own character is elevated by such laws.

The Lord indicated that the laws of His kingdom are of such high caliber that they serve to "perfect" and "sanctify" (Doctrine and Covenants 88:34) those who choose to live by them. The standards of behavior established by God's laws can elevate us to become like God as we strive to live the law He lives.

Exercising Our Agency within the Law

The Lord also explained that when we choose not to be governed by law, or not to abide the law, we can no longer be elevated or perfected by that law, nor can we expect the protections and benefits the law affords: "That which breaketh a law, and abideth not by law, but seeketh to become a law unto itself, and willeth to abide in sin, and altogether abideth in sin, cannot be sanctified by law, neither by mercy, justice, nor judgment" (Doctrine and Covenants 88:34–35).

Understanding these eternal principles of law is essential to understanding our agency and the boundaries within which we can exercise it. Law defines the sphere of our existence and agency. Without law, there can be no agency. Law is an essential element to enabling, ensuring, and protecting our agency.

When we encounter something in the law that doesn't match our own desires or makes us feel uncomfortable, we have choices to make regarding our agency:

- We can exercise our agency to change our desires and behavior to abide the law.
- We can exercise our agency to reject the law and continue in our desired behavior.
- We may seek to alter or lower the laws to match our desired behavior.
- We may choose to associate ourselves with another organization whose laws we feel better suit us, where such is available.

Obviously, each of these choices brings its own set of consequences or results. One choice not available to us is to receive the blessings, benefits, and protections which that law affords while simultaneously choosing not to abide that law ourselves. That law that seems to be an inconvenience for us when it runs contrary to our own will is the same law that provides the freedoms and protections we enjoy. We can't choose one without the other. If we choose not to live the laws of that organization, or that we will not be subject to law, then we cannot claim the benefits and protections of the law.

Can Law Be Changed?

In earthly organizations and societies, when the constituents of an organization feel that the law no longer represents their desired standard of behavior, they can work within the law to change it. However, it should be understood that changing law does have consequences. If we change the law, we alter the standard of behavior for an organization and, correspondingly, we alter the freedoms, protections, and benefits that law is able to offer. Changing law redraws the boundaries of the sphere in which agency can be exercised.

When King Mosiah established a form of democracy among the Nephites, he explained this principle of the law being determined by the voice of the people and simultaneously gave a warning, saying, "Now it is not common that the voice of the people desireth anything contrary to that which is right; but it is common for the lesser part of the people to desire that which is not right; therefore this shall ye observe and make it your law—to do your business by the voice of the people. And if the time comes that the voice of the people doth choose iniquity, then is the time that the judgments of God will come upon you" (Mosiah 29:26–27).

In earthly organizations, some changes to law are good and necessary. Laws that are unfair or inequitable don't benefit society and should absolutely be changed. Such positive changes elevate the standard and quality of life for members of that society. However, calls for changes to law are quite often not intended to elevate a society but rather to diminish the law or bring it down to a level that a broader base of society is comfortable with.

Consider, for example, the ever-evolving laws surrounding substances such as tobacco, alcohol, recreational marijuana, and other addictive substances. It would be difficult to argue that broader availability and usage of such substances beyond medicinal applications are meant to elevate society to a higher quality of life or moral character. The number of lives and livelihoods that have been destroyed through addiction to such substances is staggering. Rather, such adjustments to these laws are largely borne out of the desire to make these products more available and acceptable for use among a growing population of wanting citizens, facilitating financial markets surrounding the trade of these substances, and adapting to the limited capacity of our justice systems.

So while the laws of an earthly organization can be altered, it must be recognized that such alterations have a direct impact on the standard of behavior, quality of life, and protections and freedoms ensured for those living in that organization. Because the sphere of our existence is intertwined with the laws of that sphere, changing law directly enlarges or reduces the sphere in which we may exercise our agency.

Stability of Law

Altering law can also have significant implications on the stability of a government or organization. Members of an organization cannot maintain confidence in their government if they believe the laws are unstable. Stability of law is essential for an organization to maintain its ability to govern.

While the laws of earthly governments and organizations can and frequently do change, we learn that God's laws and His system of government are perfect and that His laws do not and will not change. He has said, "I am the Lord, I change not" (Malachi 3:6). And Moroni taught, "For do we not read that God is the same yesterday, today, and forever, and in him there is no variableness neither shadow of changing?" (Mormon 9:9). The stability of God's laws is not only essential to the stability of His kingdom, but they are also essential to our ability to confidently exercise our agency toward eternal life.

The unchanging nature of God's laws allows us to make eternal choices now, knowing that the laws and principles in God's kingdom will not change in the future. The goalpost for the character we are striving to develop through our choices will never be moved. The laws of God's kingdom we are practicing to live now are the same laws we'll be living into the eternities. Without stability of God's laws, we would not be empowered to exercise our agency to make meaningful, eternal choices and commitments today.

The Essential Role of Justice

Perhaps the most significant conflict we experience regarding our agency is accepting that our actions and choices may bring consequences that limit our privileges or opportunities. In a world with an increasing sense of entitlement, sometimes our first instinct is to rationalize that it's unfair to be denied the blessings and protections of the law even when our own behavior doesn't align with that law.

This is the struggle Corianton experienced. When Corianton violated God's law of chastity, he initially sought to rationalize that any consequences (or loss of blessings or opportunity) for his actions must be unjust or unfair. "How could it possibly be fair," his thinking may have been, "that I be punished (or denied opportunity) for my actions when everyone falls short?" Corianton unknowingly sought to "deny the justice of God" (Alma 42:20).

Is justice necessary? Can justice be avoided? What are the implications of justice on our agency?

Justice is that element of government that enforces law. Justice requires that the law be met by all constituents of a society and thus guarantees that the benefits and protections of the law are maintained.

What would happen if we removed justice from a society? It should be obvious that when law is not enforced, the law has no effect. A society without justice is a society without law. While some of God's children have experienced this firsthand, many of us can only imagine what a lawless society without justice would be like. No safety. No security. Nothing to elevate the quality of life or standard of behavior. The citizens of such a society could have no confidence whatsoever that the standards and protections established by the law would be upheld.

If the citizens of a society cannot depend on their government to administer justice to uphold the law, they quickly lose confidence in that government. Any organization or government that inconsistently implements justice, or is partial or biased in its enforcement of law, will eventually fail. Its citizens will eventually demand that government be replaced by something else, sometimes by means of physical force.

Even God's ability to maintain His kingdom, which affords its citizens so many untold opportunities and blessings, is dependent on His adherence to justice.

Alma taught Corianton, "Now the work of justice could not be destroyed; if so, God would cease to be God" (Alma 42:13).

Perhaps we don't fully appreciate how delicate this balance is as it relates to the protection of our agency. How could God possibly cease to be God? It appears that all God would need to do to lose His ability to govern would be to disregard justice, to stop enforcing the laws of His kingdom, or to play favorites regarding who is subject to justice and who is not. By doing so, God would rapidly lose the confidence of the members of His kingdom, and, as happens with earthly governments, He would cease to have the ability to govern. And if that were to occur, all the blessings and benefits of His kingdom that we've been given, including our agency, would come crumbling down.

Lehi explained this reality to his sons as follows:

> And if ye shall say there is no law, ye shall also say there is no sin. If ye shall say there is no sin, ye shall also say there is no righteousness. And if there be no righteousness there be no happiness. And if there be no righteousness nor happiness there be no punishment nor misery. And if these things are not there is no God. And if there is no God we are not, neither the earth; for there could have been no creation of things, neither to act nor to be acted upon; wherefore, all things must have vanished away. (2 Nephi 2:13)

If we rephrase the message I believe Lehi is trying to deliver, I think it might go something like the following:

"If you remove the law, then it's true there would be no notion of wrong or sin, no reason to feel guilt, and no consequences for violating the law. But if you remove the law, then you also remove the standard of existence the law provides along with all sense of right and good. And if you remove the standard of righteousness—along with its protections, blessings, and benefits provided by the law—then you also destroy agency by removing the opportunity to choose happiness and freedom. If you were to succeed in removing these things, then God would cease to be God. He would lose His kingdom. And if God ceases to be God, then all the blessings and benefits His law and kingdom provide us—including our creation, our agency, His ability to sustain life on earth, His plan of redemption, Christ's Atonement, our ability to be perfected and refined, and the Resurrection—all of these things would vanish away. And we would cease to exist because this great sphere in which He has placed us to exercise our agency would cease to exist."

So, to answer one of Corianton's potential sincere questions, can God disregard the demands of justice? Can He remove all consequence for sin? Can He simply let us choose our own standard of behavior and open the gates of His kingdom to all regardless of our willingness to abide its law? And the answer is no. Because if He does, this very delicate balance required to maintain His kingdom for our blessing and benefit disintegrates, the foundations of our existence crumble, and the opportunity for our eternal happiness is eradicated.

The Lord's statements that "no unclean thing can enter into his kingdom" (3 Nephi 27:19) and "I the Lord cannot look upon sin with the least degree of allowance" (Doctrine and Covenants 1:31) are in no way an indication that He does not love or accept us. Rather, they are an honest acknowledgment that He is required and obligated to uphold the laws of His kingdom in order to maintain the freedoms, protections, benefits, and blessings the law guarantees to its citizens.

The reality that God is required to uphold and enforce the laws of His kingdom presents an obvious challenge for us since none of us is capable of perfectly living the law. The Apostle Paul wrote, "There is none righteous, no, not one. . . . Therefore by the deeds of the law there shall no flesh be justified in his sight. . . . For all have sinned, and come short of the glory of God" (Romans 3:10, 20, 23).

Fortunately, God's plan of salvation for His children allows Him to simultaneously maintain the required principles of law and justice and still save us from the consequences of violating the law, which we all do. As we'll discuss later, the mercy extended to us through the enabling power of Christ's Atonement makes it possible for God to uphold His laws without compromising his ability to provide us with the opportunity for eternal life.

Seeking First to Understand

We've learned that our agency is fundamental to our existence. The boundaries of our agency, given to us by our Heavenly Father, are established and protected by law and upheld by the principle of justice. That agency is of the highest priority to our Heavenly Father and our Savior. They respect our agency and will never violate it. Rather, all their efforts are directed toward increasing the sphere in which we can exercise our agency.

When we encounter something in the standards and teachings of the Lord's Church on earth that is difficult for us to understand or accept, the question may arise as to whether those teachings are of God or of men. In those moments of question, how can our increased understanding of agency, law, and justice help us choose how we will exercise our agency?

We can begin by remembering how essential God's laws are to our agency. For those laws and guidelines that are given and inspired by the Lord, we can know that He has a divine purpose in them meant to benefit us. With that knowledge, we can choose to look unto Christ for increased understanding. We can sincerely ask questions such as the following: "Can you help me to understand this law? Can you help me to know where it comes from? How can living this law bless my life? Can you help me to gain a witness of this law and its purposes?" Striving to obtain that witness can help us begin to find the strength to honor God's laws even when they are dauntingly difficult for us to personally understand or accept.

Act in Faith: How Has Law Blessed Your Life?

What have you learned from our study about agency, law, and justice? How do these principles relate to your own sincere questions? To act on what we've studied, use your list of sincere questions and prayerfully consider and write down the following.

- For each question (or doubt) that you have, what laws, principles, or teachings of God's kingdom and the Church relate to your question? For example, maybe it's the law of chastity, the law of tithing, the Word of Wisdom, Christ's teachings regarding humility or repentance, or so on. Write them down alongside your question.
- How does each law or guideline serve to elevate and sanctify you as you choose to live it?
- How would your life be different if this law were not available? What would happen if each law were removed or never enforced?
- Do you understand the motivation and purpose of this law?
- Ask the Lord to help teach you how He thinks and feels about this law, to help you understand its purposes, or to help you gain a witness of its truthfulness.

Exercises

Ponder the following questions and write down your thoughts.

- Consider a serious study of the following chapters of scripture: 2 Nephi 2, Alma 42, and Doctrine and Covenants 93. What do you learn about law, justice, consequences, mercy, and agency from these chapters?

- Which of the Lord's laws or the teachings of the Church have you found most difficult to understand and live?
- What laws and teachings of the Church have most blessed your life?

Defending Our Agency

The truths we just discussed—regarding how our existence and agency are tied to God's ability to uphold the law of His kingdom and enforce the principles of justice—may seem hypothetical. However, our study of the scriptures reveals that this delicate balance is alive and at play today. Prior to our coming to earth, a great War in Heaven began over these very principles.

Regarding those events, our Heavenly Father revealed, "And [Satan] came before me, saying—Behold, here am I, send me, I will be thy son, and I will redeem all mankind, that one soul shall not be lost, and surely I will do it; wherefore give me thine honor. Wherefore, because that Satan rebelled against me, and sought to destroy the agency of man, which I, the Lord God, had given him, and also, that I should give unto him mine own power; by the power of mine Only Begotten, I caused that he should be cast down" (Moses 4:1, 3). And again, "[Satan] was angry, and kept not his first estate; and at that day, many followed after him" (Abraham 3:28).

It appears that Satan, and likely others, pitched a campaign that had the allure of redeeming all of God's children but would allegedly accomplish such without the exercise of our agency. His proposal likely included the absence of law or the absence of consequences or justice. It's obviously an attractive idea. After all, why risk not obtaining the kingdom of heaven if there's an alternative? A proposal that promises eternal life without any cost or risk is a persuasive political campaign indeed. We learn, however, that such a proposal is false and deceptive at its core.

Intuitively, we know that living an eternal, godlike life—and becoming like our heavenly parents, filled with knowledge, wisdom, love, and infinite capability—cannot be developed by any other means than though the exercise of our agency. Our level and quality of existence cannot be increased by decreasing the sphere in which we have opportunity to exercise agency. Those two things are self-contradictory by nature. Just as we can't enjoy the benefits of a driver's license if we've never had the opportunity to learn to drive, we can't master this physical tabernacle we've been given and use it to its utmost capability if we can't make choices regarding how we use it. Eternal life, for those who choose it, will be accompanied with the largest possible sphere in which we can exercise agency within the laws that accompany that sphere.

If Satan's proposal was that we'd somehow all be saved regardless of how we exercise our agency, free to act without consequences, we've examined how that is also an impossibility. Without the enforcement of law, you have only chaos and the destruction of freedom and righteousness. Removing justice results in the destruction of agency.

Satan's objective apparently had nothing to do with our well-being but rather his own desire for power, glory, and recognition. Like so many powermongers we encounter in this mortal life, Satan believed he could elevate himself by subduing the rest of us to captivity under him. Satan sought to destroy our agency and bring us into bondage under his rule for his own selfish purposes.

The Battleground Has Shifted

We know a few things regarding the outcome of that initial War in Heaven. The fact that you and I are here today is confirmation that we chose to exercise our agency to accept God's plan of salvation for His children. We accepted an increase in glory from our first estate as spirits and intelligences to our current state of glory with physical bodies. We accepted the outline of God's plan that would increase our sphere of existence and provide opportunity for us to progress. We also accepted God's structure of government, including the principles of law, justice, and mercy, as we understood them.

Unfortunately, we don't get to breathe a sigh of relief that Satan was unsuccessful in his political campaign in heaven. Recall the words of Lehi when he taught, "And I, Lehi, according to the things which I have read, must needs suppose that an angel of God, according to that which is written, had fallen from heaven; wherefore, he became a devil, having sought that which was evil before God. And because he had fallen from heaven, and had become miserable forever, he sought also the misery of all mankind" (2 Nephi 2:17–18).

And the Apostle John tells us in the book of Revelation, "And there was war in heaven: Michael and his angels fought against the dragon; and the dragon fought and his angels, And prevailed not; neither was their place found any more in heaven. And the great dragon was cast out, that old serpent, called the Devil, and Satan, which deceiveth the whole world: he was cast out into the earth, and his angels were cast out with him" (Revelation 12:7–9).

This war that Satan has waged against our agency has not ended—it has merely shifted location. Satan and those many who were drawn in by his persuasive campaign lost their first estate. They chose not to receive physical bodies and the opportunities, risks, and laws associated with this life. They were cast down as spirits to the earth, where Satan continues the war each day to "destroy the agency of man" (Moses 4:3) that the Lord our God has given us. The Savior revealed, "And thus he goeth up and down, to and fro in the earth, seeking to destroy the souls of men" (Doctrine and Covenants 10:27).

Understanding the Adversary's Approach

One must ask, "What is motivating this wayward son of God to continue this war against us?" He's obviously miserable, so perhaps he really doesn't have that much to lose. And I suppose he's still as power-hungry as he ever was. If he can bring us into captivity by getting us to use our agency to reject truth and choose something less than eternal life, then perhaps he considers that to be power, success, and glory.

But I also believe that one of Satan's largest motivators is His bitterness and anger toward our Heavenly Father and our Savior, Jesus Christ. Perhaps Satan believes he can still win this war, dethrone our

Heavenly Father, and take over the kingdom of God. I suspect he is bent on proving that God's plan of agency was a grand mistake. And if he can successfully persuade us to exercise that agency to our own destruction and condemnation, he believes he can demonstrate that he was right from the beginning. Perhaps he even believes that if he can amass a large enough army of lost souls, he can successfully launch another open rebellion against our Heavenly Father's kingdom.

Our Heavenly Father stated that "by the power of mine Only Begotten, I caused that [Satan] should be cast down" (Moses 4:3). Our Father chose Christ to fill the role of our Savior and Redeemer (see Abraham 3:27). It seems reasonable to assume that Satan views Christ as the object and cause of his demise and bears an eternal resentment and hatred toward Him. He sought to prevent the Savior's atoning sacrifice on earth and now seeks to undo the effects of Christ's Atonement in each of us individually by persuading us to choose not to accept Christ's mercy in our lives.

Why has the Lord elected to reveal Satan's motivations through scripture? Why is it worth understanding Satan's position as it relates to law, justice, consequences, mercy, and our agency? Chinese military general and strategist Sun Tzu is quoted as having said, "If you know the enemy and know yourself, you need not fear the result of a hundred battles."[53] If we can develop an awareness for how Satan goes about trying to attack our agency, we can determine how to protect and defend our agency when we recognize those attacks.

If we step into the mind of our adversary for a moment—and given what we've learned about how essential the principles of law, justice, and agency are to our existence—perhaps we can learn something by considering this hypothetical question. If we were in Satan's shoes, and had it as our goal to subject others to captivity, to take away their freedom, to reduce the sphere of their existence, and even to destroy them, how would we accomplish it?

If our existence is defined by the sphere in which we are placed to act for ourselves, the way to reduce one's existence and bring them into bondage is to find any and all means to attack their agency. We

---

53. Sun Tzu, "Attack by Stratagem," *The Art of War*, accessed Nov. 4, 2023, https://suntzusaid.com/book/3/18.

reduce the sphere in which they are able to act. There are several ways that Satan accomplishes this, but consider these three as they relate to the principles of law and justice:

- Satan attacks law. If Satan can succeed in convincing God's children that the standard of righteousness is unaccommodating, and if he succeeds in lowering the standards of law, he can reduce or erase any knowledge of the choices that would lead to eternal life. This destroys agency by making eternal life—along with the blessings, benefits, and protections of its laws—unavailable to us through ignorance. Satan does this by attacking specific laws of God meant to perfect His children but also by attacking the concept of law generally. It's worth noting that one can also attack law by attacking the character of those who give or uphold the law. It is for this reason that the adversary constantly attacks the character of God's servants on earth, hoping that reduced confidence in those servants will translate to reduced confidence in the law.
- Satan attacks justice. If Satan can succeed in removing the enforcement of law by convincing others that justice is unfair, unkind, or unnecessary, it is equivalent to removing law. Satan can simultaneously destabilize confidence in the law and government. If one succeeds in eliminating justice, they can succeed in collapsing that government. This destroys agency by removing the structure required to provide the desired protections, blessings, and benefits of the law.
- As we've already discussed, Satan attempts to make truth indistinguishable through deception and confusion. If he can create enough confusion about what is true and what is not, he can create enough noise to get God's children to exercise their agency in ways that will lead them away from truth.

Satan uses all of these tactics and more in his unceasing attempts to attack our agency. Can you recognize them at work in the world today or in your own life? Can you discern the subtle ways in which our adversary still seeks to destroy us with these methods?

Unfortunately for Lucifer, the outcome of his decisions is already known. Only more misery, and not victory, lay ahead for him. Of this heartbreaking demise Isaiah lamented:

> How art thou fallen from heaven, O Lucifer, son of the morning! how art thou cut down to the ground, which didst weaken the nations!
>
> For thou hast said in thine heart, I will ascend into heaven, I will exalt my throne above the stars of God: I will sit also upon the mount of the congregation, in the sides of the north:
>
> I will ascend above the heights of the clouds; I will be like the most High.
>
> Yet thou shalt be brought down to hell, to the sides of the pit.
>
> They that see thee shall narrowly look upon thee, and consider thee, saying, Is this the man that made the earth to tremble, that did shake kingdoms;
>
> That made the world as a wilderness, and destroyed the cities thereof; that opened not the house of his prisoners? (Isaiah 14:12–17)

I have sometimes cried when reading those verses. Here was a son of God with infinite potential who allowed his desire for power to first blind him to the happiness he might have obtained and then motivate him to take so many others with him. This must be heartbreaking for our Heavenly Father. And although Satan has chosen something truly destructive to himself and other children of God, even he has not lost the love of our Heavenly Father, who surely still weeps over this fallen son of glory.

What is not yet determined is what *we* will choose. The battle for each of our souls individually is still very much in play. In the next chapter, we're going to outline the beautiful structure of the kingdom God has prepared for us. We're going to study what our options and opportunities are. As we study those glorious truths, we'll see the love our Heavenly Father has for us, the great respect He has for our agency, and Christ's willingness to do whatever it takes to bring us home.

Act in Faith

Using the laws you identified in the last chapter that relate to your sincere questions, consider the following.

- Has Satan sought to attack your agency regarding any of these laws? If so, how?
- What evidences do you observe that Satan's war against our agency continues today, as evidenced by his attacks on law and justice?

The Kingdom of God

We've discussed how law defines and protects the sphere in which we are able to exercise our agency and enjoy promised blessings and benefits. Law elevates and lifts the members of a society by establishing a standard of behavior. We also learned that God cannot change or compromise the laws of His kingdom while still maintaining its stability.

However, we also know by our own experience that not all of God's children want to live the same law. Although our Heavenly Father sincerely desires to give us all that He has—and enable us to live the same kind of life He lives, with its accompanying capacity for joy—He recognizes that we may exercise our agency to choose something else. How then is God able to provide a place for all of His children in His kingdom where they can each have joy in what they most desire, without lowering or changing the laws of His kingdom to accommodate our individual desires?

Recall again these words from the Savior that we studied previously: "And there are many kingdoms, for there is no space in the which there is no kingdom; and there is no kingdom in which there is no space, either a greater or a lesser kingdom. And unto every kingdom is given a law; and unto every law there are certain bounds also and conditions" (Doctrine and Covenants 88:37–38).

Our Heavenly Father's plan for us provides "many kingdoms," with each kingdom having a different level of law. With this structure, God lovingly provides us the opportunity to choose what level of law we are willing to abide and what kind of society and environment we are most comfortable with.

What are these kingdoms? Of course, most Church members are familiar with them. We've been taught them since our youth or from the missionary lessons we received before our baptism. The Prophet Joseph Smith and Sidney Rigdon were shown these kingdoms in a vision. We find their description of that vision in Doctrine and Covenants 76: "And the glory of the celestial is one, even as the glory of the sun is one. And the glory of the terrestrial is one, even as the glory of the moon is one. And the glory of the telestial is one, even as the glory of the stars is one; for as one star differs from another star in glory, even so differs one from another in glory in the telestial world" (Doctrine and Covenants 76:96–98).

Our Heavenly Father describes each of the celestial, terrestrial, and telestial kingdoms as being kingdoms of glory. Here again we see the Lord's use of terms relating to light (the sun, moon, and stars) as an analogy. When we see the word *glory* in these verses, we can think of this as a particular level intelligence, light, and truth associated with each kingdom, with the celestial kingdom being the highest. Correspondingly, each kingdom has a different set of laws and provides a different level of freedom, benefits, and opportunity.

The Lord has revealed that the kingdom to which we will enter after the Resurrection will be our choosing based on the level of law that we desire and are willing to live. After referring to those who are sanctified through Christ's Atonement to inherit a celestial glory, the Lord revealed, "And they who are not sanctified through the law which I have given unto you, even the law of Christ, must inherit another kingdom, even that of a terrestrial kingdom, or that of a telestial kingdom. For he who is not able to abide the law of a celestial kingdom cannot abide a celestial glory. And he who cannot abide the law of a terrestrial kingdom cannot abide a terrestrial glory" (Doctrine and Covenants 88:21–23).

And so the Lord has made available to us three options, kingdoms, or spaces in which we can choose to live. Although the Lord has not revealed all the details of each of these kingdoms and their associated laws, He has given us some information. Let's look at each one briefly.

The Celestial Kingdom

The celestial kingdom provides the largest possible "sphere" in which God can place us to exercise our agency, and thus the highest possible level of existence that we can obtain (see Doctrine and Covenants 93:30). While the celestial kingdom provides the greatest degree of freedom, it also comes with the corresponding highest law and standards of behavior and discipline. Here are some of the details the Lord has revealed regarding the requirements, blessings, and qualities of those of His children who choose to live a celestial law:

- They receive the testimony of Jesus (see Doctrine and Covenants 76:51).
- They believe on Jesus's name (see verse 51).
- They receive baptism by authority (see verse 51).
- They keep the commandments (see verse 52).
- They receive the Holy Spirit by the laying on of hands of authorized priesthood holders (see verse 52).
- They overcome by faith (see verse 53).
- They are just and true (see verse 53).
- They receive the laws and ordinances of the Melchizedek Priesthood (see verse 57).
- They enter into the everlasting covenant of marriage. (Note that this is only required to enter the highest degree of the celestial kingdom—see Doctrine and Covenants 131:1–4.)
- They are washed and cleansed from all their sins (see verse 52).
- They are sealed by the Holy Spirit of promise (see verse 53).
- They become the Church of the Firstborn (see verse 54).
- The Father gives all things into their hands (see verse 55).
- They become priests and kings, priestesses and queens (see verse 56).
- They receive the fulness and glory of the Father (see verse 56).
- They are gods, even the sons of God (see verse 58; see also Doctrine and Covenants 132:20).

- All things are theirs (see verse 59).
- They shall overcome all things (see verse 60).
- They shall dwell in the presence of God and Christ forever and ever (see verse 62).
- They shall come with Christ when He reigns over the earth (see verse 63).
- They have part in the first Resurrection (see verse 64).
- They come forth in the Resurrection of the just (see verse 65).
- Their names are written in heaven (see verse 68).
- They are just men and women made perfect through Christ's Atonement (see verse 69).
- They receive celestial bodies like our Heavenly Father (see verse 70).
- They shall possess the earth after it is cleansed and sanctified (see Doctrine and Covenants 88:17–20).
- They may "inherit thrones, kingdoms, principalities, and powers, dominions, all heights and depths" (Doctrine and Covenants 132:19).

Those are just a few of the descriptions the Lord has provided regarding the requirements and blessings of those who choose to live a celestial law. This is the kingdom and sphere of existence in which our Heavenly Father resides. God abides a celestial law and enjoys all the freedoms and blessings associated with that law. He makes that same level of existence available to all of His children who desire and are willing to live that same life and are made capable and worthy of doing so through the redeeming power of Jesus Christ's Atonement.

We should pause here to make note of the Lord's laws regarding marriage in the celestial kingdom. Celestial law defines marriage as being between man and woman (see Doctrine and Covenants 132:19).[54] Marriage is a requirement for those who choose to enter into the highest degree of the celestial kingdom (see Doctrine and Covenants 131:1–4). However, marriage is not a requirement to live a celestial law. There are many of God's children who will choose to

54. See also "The Family: A Proclamation to the World," Gospel Library.

live the celestial kingdom's law of chastity but who may choose not to enter into the covenant of marriage.

We should also note that the Lord has not revealed details regarding the laws of the terrestrial or telestial kingdoms regarding marriage covenants or commitments that don't adhere to the definition of marriage as defined by celestial law. The Lord has also not revealed any details regarding the nature of our resurrected physical bodies as it relates to sexual attraction.

The Terrestrial Kingdom

While He has not directly revealed details surrounding terrestrial law, God has revealed some details regarding the qualities of those of His children who choose to live this law:

- Their glory differs from those who receive the fulness of the Father in the celestial kingdom (see Doctrine and Covenants 76:71).
- Among them are those who "died without law," meaning they did not have the gospel of Jesus Christ in life because they chose not to accept it after having a fair opportunity to understand and receive it (see verses 72 and 74).
- They accepted the gospel of Jesus Christ after this life (again, after having rejected it in this life) (see verse 74).
- They were honorable men and women on earth but were blinded by the craftiness of men (see verse 75).
- They receive of God's glory but not of His fulness (see verse 76).
- They enjoy the presence of Jesus Christ but not the fulness of Heavenly Father (see verse 77).
- Their resurrected bodies are terrestrial and not celestial in nature (see verse 78).
- They are not "valiant" in the testimony of Jesus (see verse 79).

The Telestial Kingdom

The Lord has also given a few details regarding the nature and circumstances of those who choose to live a telestial law rather than a terrestrial or celestial law:

- Their glory is less than those of the terrestrial or celestial kingdom (Doctrine and Covenants 76:81).
- They rejected the gospel of Jesus Christ both in this life and after this life (see verse 82).
- They deny not the Holy Ghost (see verse 83). They do not deny the truth and validity of God's plan of salvation, Christ's Atonement, or the justice and mercy of God once they have understood such. This is in contrast to those individuals who receive a firm understanding of God's plan and choose to rebel or reject it entirely, as Lucifer and his followers have done.
- They shall come forth in the last Resurrection (see verse 85).
- They receive not of Christ's fulness but do enjoy the ministration of the Holy Ghost (see verse 86).
- They are servants of God but cannot go where God and Christ dwell (see verse 112).
- They are ministered to by those in the terrestrial kingdom (see verse 86).
- They receive the administering of angels appointed to minister for them (see verse 88).
- They too are heirs of salvation (see verse 88).
- Joseph Smith and Sidney Rigdon indicated that even the glory of the telestial kingdom "surpasses all understanding" (see verse 89).
- The inhabitants of the telestial world are "as innumerable as the stars" or "the sand upon the seashore" (see verse 109).

These descriptions of the telestial kingdom would suggest that although it is the lowest of our Heavenly Father's kingdoms in terms of law and glory, its quality of life far exceeds that which we experience in this mortal life. Elder James E. Talmage taught that "all who receive of any one of these orders of glory are at last saved, and upon them Satan will finally have no claim."[55] The scriptural descriptions also suggest that a great many of Heavenly Father's children will choose to abide the laws of this kingdom.

Choices outside the Kingdom of God

There is, evidently, another option we may choose beyond the three kingdoms of glory our Heavenly Father has prepared for us. As we've already discussed, Heavenly Father never forces anything upon us. He does not govern by oppression or force but by invitation, love, and persuasion (see Doctrine and Covenants 121:41–46). We may, if we so choose, essentially "opt out" of God's kingdom entirely. The following verses describe this option:

> And he who cannot abide the law of a telestial kingdom cannot abide a telestial glory; therefore he is not meet for a kingdom of glory. Therefore he must abide a kingdom which is not a kingdom of glory. . . . And they who remain shall also be quickened; nevertheless, they shall return again to their own place, to enjoy that which they are willing to receive, because they were not willing to enjoy that which they might have received. (Doctrine and Covenants 88:24, 32)

The Lord does not reveal what, if any, place is made available for those who decide they do not want to receive the blessings and benefits of any of God's kingdoms with their accompanying laws. I suppose that very few of God's children will select this option, unwilling to abide any law. Such an option may effectively leave us to our own devices to subsist in the universe. The laws of the celestial, terrestrial, and telestial kingdoms combined should provide ample opportunity for nearly all of our Heavenly Father's children to identify the type of life and law they are willing to receive and enjoy into the eternities.

Our Agency to Choose

"How will I know which kingdom I'm going to receive when I'm resurrected?" That's a common question many Latter-day Saints ponder. In reality, we don't have to wonder. The kingdom of glory

---

55. James E. Talmage, *The Articles of Faith*, 12th ed. [1924], 91–92.

that we will ultimately enter into is not a pending decision by our Heavenly Father but rather a choice that each of us can make today and throughout our life.

Elder David A. Bednar, in speaking to youth in South America, shared the following thought: "You don't have to die to find out [where you're going]. . . . The Lord is not going to have to tell you. When you come into His presence, you will go where you know you belong, based on what we have desired to do and become while we have lived on the earth."[56]

Elder Bednar shared the idea that the kingdom we enter into will be a reflection of the law we have learned to love. We will ultimately be surrounded with other people who desire to live the same level of law that we desire to live.

However, as we've already discussed, many Church members' concern regarding their relationship with the Savior and whether they will receive eternal life is not that they don't desire it but that they won't be worthy or "good enough" to receive it. And that is where the mercy offered by Jesus Christ completes our Heavenly Father's plan, which we'll study in the next chapter.

The Kingdom of God on Earth

President Dallin H. Oaks taught, "The work of The Church of Jesus Christ of Latter-day Saints is ultimately concerned with preparing the children of God for the celestial kingdom, and most particularly for its highest glory, exaltation or eternal life."[57]

The Church of Jesus Christ of Latter-day Saints, as the Lord's restored Church on the earth bearing His name and priesthood authority, is primarily focused on preparing God's children to live a celestial law. Thus, the Church strives for celestial standards of living in its doctrines, policies, and teachings, affirming that these are given under the direction of Jesus Christ through revelation to His authorized prophets and apostles.

---

56. David A. Bednar, in "Preguntas y Respuestas con Elder Bednar," Iglesia de Jesucristo, Feb. 23, 2016, video, 1:52:50, https://www.youtube.com/live/NnIr53ZHYVg?si=ZOVft4vGMsHyPyuB.

57. Dallin H. Oaks, "*Two* Great Commandments," *Ensign*, Nov. 2019, 74.

A common challenge arises when individuals struggle to reconcile (1) the Church's responsibility to proactively and unapologetically teach eternal truths of God's laws in preparation for eternal life and (2) the Church's teachings regarding unconditional love and respect for all of God's children, regardless of the law they choose to live. In a society that continually trends further away from the standards of celestial law, an increasing number of God's children may misinterpret the Church's obligation to uphold God's laws as a lack of empathy, acceptance, or love for those who disagree with them.

As members of the Church, we can each strive to help each other know we have a place in God's kingdom on earth and in heaven. We can seek to honor the feelings of Christ toward all of God's children as Nephi beautifully described:

> He doeth not anything save it be for the benefit of the world; for he loveth the world, even that he layeth down his own life that he may draw all men unto him. Wherefore, he commandeth none that they shall not partake of his salvation.
>
> Behold, doth he cry unto any, saying: Depart from me? Behold, I say unto you, Nay; but he saith: Come unto me all ye ends of the earth, buy milk and honey, without money and without price.
>
> Behold, hath he commanded any that they should depart out of the synagogues, or out of the houses of worship? Behold, I say unto you, Nay.
>
> Hath he commanded any that they should not partake of his salvation? Behold I say unto you, Nay; but he hath given it free for all men; and he hath commanded his people that they should persuade all men to repentance.
>
> Behold, hath the Lord commanded any that they should not partake of his goodness? Behold I say unto you, Nay; but all men are privileged the one like unto the other, and none are forbidden. (2 Nephi 26:24–28)

The highest form of love we can show for God's children does not come from shying away from the truths of the gospel or by apologizing for the doctrine of Christ and God's laws. Instead, it comes by inviting all to come unto Christ, to know of His laws and truths, and to experience Christ's love and redeeming power in their lives. We have the opportunity to share what we know about how God can prepare us to live a godlike life and the joy and opportunities made available to us.

As we do so, we must strive to demonstrate the same unconditional love and understanding that our Heavenly Father has for each of His children. We can strive to show great empathy for those whose struggle to accept and live Christ's restored gospel is more difficult than our own. And this we can do while completely respecting the agency of God's children. We can respect everyone's right to disagree with our views, and we can do so in a spirit of love and understanding.

Act in Faith: How Do Your Questions Prepare You for God's Kingdom?

For each of your doubts or sincere questions you've listed, consider the following.

- How does this question relate to the laws and blessings associated with the kingdom of our Heavenly Father that you desire to live?
- How will the answer to this question help prepare you for the kingdom you desire to receive?

Redeemed through the Mercy of Jesus Christ

We've learned that justice is an essential principle in the kingdom of God. Without adherence to justice, God would "cease to be God" and all the blessings and benefits of His kingdom, including our own lives and existence, would come to an end (see Alma 42:13, 22; 2 Nephi 2:13).

However, justice demands strict adherence to the law—without exceptions. And yet each of us falls short of a celestial law on a regular basis. None of us, as we currently are, is worthy and capable of fully living a celestial law. Our sins and fallen nature make it impossible for us to merit entrance into the kingdom of God and His presence if we're left entirely subject to the demands of justice.

So if justice must be satisfied for the law to be upheld, how then can we be saved when we are presently incapable of living the demands of a celestial law? How can we hope to inherit the blessings our Heavenly Father enjoys from living a godlike life when we constantly fall short through sin and mistakes and when our natural desires often lead us to seek something far less than our potential? The answer, of course, is through the mercy made available to us through the Atonement of Jesus Christ.

Made Free through Jesus Christ

Christ's atoning sacrifice is that critical element in our Heavenly Father's plan that can not only rescue us from the cold demands of justice but also transform us into beings capable of living any type of law we desire to live. Ultimately, our freedom to choose our destiny is only made possible through Jesus Christ. Otherwise, we would be entirely subject to the demands of justice and the consequences of the law, and we would all be forever shut out of the presence of God, unable to reach our potential for joy and happiness.

Alma explained this to Corianton, saying, "And now, the plan of mercy could not be brought about except an Atonement should be made; therefore God himself atoneth for the sins of the world, to bring about the plan of mercy, to appease the demands of justice, that God might be a perfect, just God, and a merciful God also" (Alma 42:15).

Christ, because of His character and His unique role and position in the kingdom of our Heavenly Father, was able to step between us and the demands of justice and suffer the full consequences for our sins and shortcomings. His sacrifice fully satisfied the demands of justice upon us. Christ's Atonement was sufficient to enact the law of mercy in the plan of our Heavenly Father on our behalf, thus ultimately freeing us from all mortal limitations and making it possible for us to choose eternal life.

Lehi explained this glorious truth to his sons, saying:

> And the Messiah cometh in the fulness of time, that he may redeem the children of men from the fall. And because that they are redeemed from the fall they have become free forever, knowing good from evil; to act for themselves and not to be acted upon, save it be by the punishment of the law at the great and last day, according to the commandments which God hath given.
>
> Wherefore, men are free according to the flesh; and all things are given them which are expedient unto man. And they are free to choose liberty and eternal life, through the great Mediator of all men, or to choose captivity and death, according to the captivity and power of the devil. (2 Nephi 2:26–27)

The mercy made available to us through Christ's atoning sacrifice truly makes us free! Free to choose whatever it is we most want to become.

Equality in Christ

Jesus Christ is the great equalizer in our Heavenly Father's plan. We all know that this mortal life is not fair. None of us are born into the same circumstances and opportunities as anyone else. Some of our Heavenly Father's children experience far more severe trials, temptations, and challenges than others. And some of our Heavenly Father's children find faith much more difficult to develop than others.

Comparatively, my own life has been relatively devoid of the severe struggles of faith that many of my spiritual brothers and sisters have had to pass through in this life. I've not yet had to face the experiences of same-sex attraction, or a severe battle with mental or physical health challenges, or the crushing blow of a failed marriage, or severe economic disadvantage, or the oppression of tyranny, or devastating natural disaster, or the horrors of physical, emotional, or sexual abuse. No, in the school of hard knocks, I likely have not yet earned even a participation award, let alone a passing grade.

And so none of us, especially not me, is in a position to pass judgment on one of our brothers or sisters as it pertains to their choices and their wrestle with doubt as they try to navigate this mortal journey.

But I do have a sure, personal witness that Christ's infinite mercy and Atonement are able to make all things right and fair and just in the end, regardless of how inequitable our life here may be. As Nephi taught, "He inviteth them all to come unto him and partake of his goodness; and he denieth none that come unto him, black and white, bond and free, male and female . . . and all are alike unto God" (2 Nephi 26:33).

Whatever our disadvantages in this life, Christ will ultimately level the playing field such that each of us has a full and comprehensive opportunity to understand and accept His offer to save us from sin, pain, ignorance, mortal temptation, and infirmity. And as we accept His offer, our opportunity to receive eternal life will be determined not by our capability but only by what we most desire.

Christ's Condition: Meekness

Christ taught, "And my Father sent me that I might be lifted up upon the cross; and after that I had been lifted up upon the cross, that I might draw all men unto me. . . . And for this cause have I been lifted up; therefore, according to the power of the Father I will draw all men unto me" (3 Nephi 27:14–15).

Christ, having fully satisfied the demands of justice, draws us unto Him, and He effectively becomes our new creditor. Instead of requiring a flawless performance from us, as justice does, Christ is able to turn to us and offer a new deal. And He only asks one thing from us. He has said, "My grace is sufficient for all men that humble themselves before me; for if they humble themselves before me, and have faith in me, then will I make weak things become strong unto them" (Ether 12:27).

Christ's only object is our salvation. And because He is infinitely capable, He only needs one thing from us to enable Him to save us, and that is our will. If we can give up our will and become teachable, meek, and humble, He will help us do all the rest.

Recall again this plea and promise from our Savior indicating His requirement of humility along with his commitment to save us: "And ye shall offer for a sacrifice unto me a broken heart and a contrite spirit. And whoso cometh unto me with a broken heart and a contrite spirit, him will I baptize with fire and with the Holy Ghost. Therefore, whoso repenteth and cometh unto me as a little child, him will I receive, for of such is the kingdom of God. Behold, for such I have laid down my life, and have taken it up again; therefore repent, and come unto me ye ends of the earth, and be saved" (3 Nephi 9:21–22).

There is nothing Christ cannot do with us. If Christ can change water into wine, then certainly He can change our hearts, our minds, and even the chemistry of our bodies to be capable of living a celestial life. He can change us to overcome addiction, the pain of abuse, the scars of sin, and even the desire to sin (though we know some of those changes may not occur until after this life on earth). However, because Christ fiercely advocates for and defends our agency, even to the sacrificing of His own life to ensure it, He will not change us against our will. We have to choose to submit to Him.

The Glory of God's Plan

And here we must pause and reflect on the great and glorious plan our Heavenly Father has created for us. God's only intent is our well-being. He seeks to bring about our immortality and eternal life (see Moses 1:39). He lovingly gave us the opportunity to increase from our original state of light and truth to an increased existence of agency, freedom, and opportunity. He accomplishes this through eternal principles of sanctifying law, justice, and agency.

He's created a space for each of us where we can ultimately have whatever we most desire, and live whatever type of law we're most comfortable with. And because we're not ready to live a celestial law and we fall short, He has rescued us from the demands of justice in His own kingdom by sending His Only Begotten Son in the flesh, Jesus Christ, who willfully offered Himself as a sacrifice to make mercy an option for us.

God's plan is fully comprehensive and inclusive. None of us is excluded. We all fit in and have a place in the kingdom of our Heavenly Father, whatever place we choose—even being in His presence and enjoying the same kind of life that He enjoys if we so desire.

Surely it is this realization that caused Nephi to exclaim, "I glory in my Jesus, for he hath redeemed my soul" (2 Nephi 33:6), and Alma to rejoice, "I know that he will raise me up at the last day, to dwell with him in glory; yea, and I will praise him forever" (Alma 36:28). And again, Nephi proclaimed, "My soul delighteth in the covenants of the Lord . . . yea, my soul delighteth in his grace, and in his justice, and power, and mercy in the great and eternal plan of deliverance" (2 Nephi 11:5).

Choosing Mercy

We began our discussion of agency with the concerns expressed by Alma's son, Corianton. Alma taught Corianton that peace and happiness don't come by trying to rationalize away the reality of God's laws or the requirements of justice. Instead, they come by looking to Christ and accepting the infinite mercy He makes available to us through His atoning sacrifice. After Alma explained the principles of agency, law, justice, and mercy to Corianton, he counseled, "O my son, I desire that ye should deny the justice of God no more. Do not endeavor to excuse yourself in the least point because of your sins, by denying the justice of God; but do you let the justice of God, and his mercy, and his long-suffering have full sway in your heart; and let it bring you down to the dust in humility" (Alma 42:30).

When our fears similarly lead to doubts—feelings that the bar is set too high, that our persistent shortcomings and temptations render us incapable or unworthy of living a godlike life, or that we don't fit into the kingdom of God—we can choose to look unto Christ in those thoughts and replace doubt with a personal witness of the mercy made available to us through the redeeming power of His Atonement. No matter how far from the standard of celestial law we may currently be, Christ has the power to cleanse us, change us, sanctify us, and make us worthy of and prepared for eternal life in the kingdom of our Father. Our God is a "perfect, just God, and a merciful God also" (Alma 42:15).

Act in Faith: Applying Christ's Mercy to Our Agency

For each of your sincere questions or doubts, ponder and write down the following.

- What choices are available to me regarding this doubt or question? How does God expect me to exercise my agency in regard to this question?
- How does Christ's Atonement influence my ability to choose regarding this question?
- How can Christ change me in regard to this question?
- As I ponder this question, what is it I most want? How can I exercise my agency combined with Christ's redeeming power to obtain what I most want?

Recognizing Answers and Waiting on the Lord

If you have made it this far and have put into practice the principles we've discussed, you have exercised tremendous faith. You've (1) exercised your agency to seek the Lord's voice through the Holy Ghost, (2) remembered God's mercy for you and His children, (3) converted your doubts into sincere questions, (4) recalled the spiritual witnesses of truth you've received throughout your life, (5) sought the help of priesthood leaders, (6) identified ideal sources to study in your search for truth, (7) gone to the Lord in sincere prayer asking for help and guidance, (8) repented of sins, (9) sought to understand and live the commandments and principles of the gospel, and (10) studied to understand and embrace the beautiful gift of agency made available to us through the redeeming power of Jesus Christ. Is not this "exceedingly great faith?" (Alma 13:3).

I hope that you've been receiving answers from heaven as you've sincerely tried to implement these principles. I hope you're able to recognize the voice of the Holy Ghost guiding you to the knowledge you need in order to move forward in faith. I hope you're having revelatory, life-changing personal experiences with our Heavenly Father and our Savior. I hope you've felt Their love for you.

Our first principle was to understand that the answers to the most important questions of our souls can come only from heaven by revelation through the Holy Ghost. That is the surest witness any of us can receive in this life. As we now draw to the end of our study, we'll end where we began, seeking to recognize the voice of the Holy Ghost and the answers our Heavenly Father wants to give us. How will the answers come? How can we recognize the voice of the Lord when He speaks to us?

Entire books are dedicated to the subject of receiving revelation and recognizing the voice of the Spirit. Here we'll only touch on a few points as they pertain to our sincere search for answers. As we do so, try to identify the answers the Lord may have already given you as you've acted in faith on the principles we've discussed.

The Mind and Heart

The Lord gave this counsel to Oliver Cowdery when teaching him how to discern revelation: "Yea, behold, I will tell you in your mind and in your heart, by the Holy Ghost, which shall come upon you and which shall dwell in your heart. Now, behold, this is the spirit of revelation" (Doctrine and Covenants 8:2–3).

The Savior similarly taught this principle to Hyrum Smith using these words: "Verily, verily, I say unto you, I will impart unto you of my Spirit, which shall enlighten your mind, which shall fill your soul with joy; And then shall ye know, or by this shall you know, all things whatsoever you desire of me" (Doctrine and Covenants 11:13–14).

In these verses, the Lord explains that the Holy Ghost speaks to our mind and our heart. Speaking to the mind implies conveying knowledge, information, and understanding. The word *enlighten* means to give greater knowledge, especially knowledge of a spiritual nature.

This is likely the most common form of revelation. Thoughts and ideas spoken to our mind by the Holy Ghost occur more frequently than we recognize. Joseph Smith taught, "A person may profit by noticing the first intimation of the spirit of revelation; for instance, when you feel pure intelligence flowing into you, it may give you sudden strokes of ideas."[58]

As you have acted in faith on the principles we've shared, have you found your thoughts carried away into productive ideas or promptings to help you find answers to your questions?

You'll recall the experience of my friend Beth as she sought a witness of the Book of Mormon. After a few weeks of striving to receive that witness, Beth began asking the Lord if there was anything more she needed to do. She asked if there was anything preventing her from receiving an answer. One day, while listening to a conference talk and doing her hair, she received a distinct impression that she needed to give up watching television, at least for a while.

Beth recalled, "I had certain shows that I loved watching. Giving up TV was not something I wanted to do. It was part of my nightly routine after successfully getting through another day. I decided to go forth with it."

Your own promptings may not include giving up television, but if you have been receiving personal promptings from the Holy Ghost during your struggle with doubt, embrace them! Act on them! Those promptings are direct guidance from heaven tailored to your unique experience, and miracles follow when we act on them.

The Savior's words also indicate that the Spirit will speak to our "heart" and "soul." Revelation is often accompanied with feelings, emotions, comfort, or conviction. When the Holy Ghost speaks to us, we often not only learn something intellectually but experience something spiritually. This combination of both mind and heart has a way of burning the truth into our souls so that it becomes part of us and is not easily undone.

Beth's experience is an example of the Spirit speaking to the mind and heart. She received knowledge and understanding. She was guided by the Spirit along the way as to what she could do to receive answers to her prayers. She received an answer to the question she'd been asking. Her mind was "enlightened." But the message wasn't just communicated to Beth's mind; her heart was also touched. Both Beth

58. *History of the Church*, 3:381; from a discourse given by Joseph Smith on June 27, 1839, in Commerce, Illinois; reported by Willard Richards.

and her bishop were filled with joy. Such experiences often accompany the teaching of the Holy Ghost.

Act in Faith: How Has the Spirit Spoken to Your Mind and Heart?

As you have acted in faith on the principles we've discussed, how has the Holy Ghost enlightened your mind? What ideas and promptings have you received directing you on your way in your search for answers? Are any of these thoughts and ideas answers to your sincere questions? What spiritual experiences have you had when the Spirit has touched your heart or brought joy to your soul through this process? Take a moment to recognize these and write them down.

The Spirit Edifies

In the early days of the restored Church, there were questions among Church members as to whether certain spiritual manifestations were from God or from other sources. To help the Saints distinguish the Holy Ghost from other spirits, the Savior taught this principle: "Therefore, why is it that ye cannot understand and know, that he that receiveth the word by the Spirit of truth receiveth it as it is preached by the Spirit of truth? Wherefore, he that preacheth and he that receiveth, understand one another, and both are edified and rejoice together. And that which doth not edify is not of God, and is darkness" (Doctrine and Covenants 50:21–23).

When we are taught by the Spirit of truth, we receive both understanding and edification. To *edify* means to improve, to uplift, to benefit, or to build up. Conversely, the Lord explained that those things that do not build us up or encourage us to become more like God are not of Him.

Beth's countenance changed through her experience of striving to receive a witness of the gospel. She became happier. Her self-confidence improved. Her relationship with the Savior became more evident in her appearance. She was being edified, built up, and made better.

As we have been studying the principles of overcoming doubt and acting in faith, have you felt a desire to become better, nobler, kinder, or closer to God and Jesus Christ, along with confidence that you can?

If so, those promptings are revelation from the Holy Ghost. When we experience those thoughts and feelings, we can take courage in knowing that the Holy Ghost is working in our lives and that our prayers are being answered.

Act in Faith: How Have You Been Edified?

In what ways have you felt edified, built up, or drawn closer to God as you've demonstrated your faith through acting on these principles? As you've sought out resources to study in search of answers to your questions, which of those sources have edified you and which have made you feel more distant from God? Make note of these along with your questions. That edifying Spirit is one way the Lord provides answers to our sincere questions.

The Spirit Leadeth to Do Good

The Holy Ghost motivates us to behave and act in positive ways. The Lord taught, "And now, verily, verily, I say unto thee, put your trust in that Spirit which leadeth to do good—yea, to do justly, to walk humbly, to judge righteously; and this is my Spirit" (Doctrine and Covenants 11:12).

Revelation from the Spirit motivates us to do good and to be good. When a holy member of the Godhead reaches out to pull us upward, we become a little more holy ourselves. Our desires and motives change, and we feel a desire to be better and more Christlike to all around us. The Holy Ghost gradually sanctifies us.

After Beth's experiences confirming her witness of the gospel, she began to make significant changes in the way she spent her time. She began reaching out more to serve widows and other young mothers in her ward. Whenever the Bishop would visit a family in the ward, he would often find that Beth had recently been a blessing to them in some way. She was more given to serve in callings. She gave up hobbies and activities in her life that she thought might be leading her away from the Spirit. These were all effects of "that Spirit which leadeth to do good."

Act in Faith: How Has the Spirit Motivated You to Do Good?

As you've been working through the principles in this book, what good has the Spirit motivated you to do? These may have been promptings to pray, to reach out to someone in need, to serve someone, to repent of sins, to be more kind, or to ask for forgiveness. Make note of these promptings and try to connect them back to your acts of faith. These promptings are another form of answers from heaven in response to sincere questions.

The Fruits of the Spirit

Perhaps there are no verses more frequently quoted regarding the feelings the Holy Ghost brings than these from the Apostle Paul: "But the fruit of the Spirit is love, joy, peace, longsuffering, gentleness, goodness, faith, meekness, temperance: against such there is no law" (Galatians 5:22–23).

These feelings and attributes attend one who is receiving divine truth from the Holy Ghost. These feelings can occur in the very moment we are being taught by the Spirit, but they are also the cumulative effects of the Holy Ghost on our character. The Holy Ghost gradually changes us to become more loving, joyful, peaceful, longsuffering, gentle, good, faithful, meek, and temperate.

Conversely, when we experience feelings of hatred, selfish sorrow, fear, impatience, brashness, unkindness, doubt, pride, envy, or intemperance, we may know that the spirit trying to influence us is not of God but some other spirit.

Act in Faith: What Fruits of the Spirit Are You Experiencing?

As you've been seeking answers to your sincere questions, what fruits of the Spirit have you observed in yourself or others? When have you felt love, joy, peace, or patience? Have you felt to be more kind, humble, and teachable? Has the Spirit been gradually changing you to reflect these attributes? Make note of these moments and the changes you've been experiencing.

Did Not Our Hearts Burn within Us?

One of my favorite accounts of the Savior teaching by the Spirit occurred on the glorious day of His Resurrection in the Holy Land. Two of His disciples were on the road from Jerusalem to a village called Emmaus when the resurrected Savior joined them on their journey. The scriptures tell us that His disciples did not recognize Him, for "their eyes were holden that they should not know him" (Luke 24:16).

These two disciples had a very personal and touching experience with their Lord and Master. Here it is as recorded in the book of Luke:

> And beginning at Moses and all the prophets, [Jesus] expounded unto them in all the scriptures the things concerning himself.
>
> And they drew nigh unto the village, whither they went: and he made as though he would have gone further.
>
> But they constrained him, saying, Abide with us: for it is toward evening, and the day is far spent. And he went in to tarry with them.
>
> And it came to pass, as he sat at meat with them, he took bread, and blessed it, and brake, and gave to them.
>
> And their eyes were opened, and they knew him; and he vanished out of their sight.
>
> And they said one to another, Did not our heart burn within us, while he talked with us by the way, and while he opened to us the scriptures? (Luke 24:27–32)

What a wonderful experience! How would it be to be taught face to face by the resurrected Savior and to have Him personally administer the bread as a symbol of His atoning sacrifice? You would think those experiences alone would have been sufficient to make them recognize the Savior. But note the evidence these disciples used to confirm that it was indeed Him: "Did not our heart burn within us?" (Luke 24:32). It was the personal witness borne to their hearts by the Holy Ghost that convinced them they had been with Jesus.

The Savior explained this method by which the Holy Ghost bears witness of truth when instructing Oliver Cowdery on how to translate the Book of Mormon: "Behold, I say unto you, that you must study it out in your mind; then you must ask me if it be right, and if it is right I will cause that your bosom shall burn within you; therefore, you shall feel that it is right" (Doctrine and Covenants 9:8).

Many members of the Church have experienced this "burning in the bosom." But it's important to know that not everybody describes or experiences this form of revelation the same way. President Dallin H. Oaks gave the following explanation: "What does a 'burning in the bosom' mean? Does it need to be a feeling of caloric heat, like the burning produced by combustion? If that is the meaning, I have never had a burning in the bosom. Surely, the word 'burning' in this scripture signifies a feeling of comfort and serenity. That is the witness many receive. That is the way revelation works."[59]

Many faithful Saints wonder if they have experienced this form of revelation. I have personally learned that I most often experience this when the Spirit is trying to confirm the truthfulness of something being said by someone else. I've had many moments listening to talks in sacrament meetings or from Church leaders when I've felt this confirming witness that what they were teaching was true. The Spirit seemed to be "burning" the teaching into my mind and heart, making it part of me, permanently changing my perspective and understanding. Over time, I have become better at identifying when it is taking place.

Act in Faith: When Has the Spirit Confirmed Truth to Your Heart?

As you have sought answers to questions through sincere study, have there been moments when your heart has "burned within you," as Jesus's disciples described? Such experiences can be answers to prayer as the Spirit confirms the truth to our hearts. Write these down alongside your questions.

How Does the Spirit Speak to You Personally?

We've studied the words of our Savior and His servants as they have tried to articulate how the Holy Ghost communicates with us. These explanations can help us to recognize the voice of the Spirit

---

59. Dallin H. Oaks, "Teaching and Learning by the Spirit", *Ensign*, March 1997, 13.

when we experience it. But each of us needs to learn for ourselves how the Spirit uniquely communicates with us. Consider these few ways you can act in faith to increase your ability to recognize the voice of the Spirit as He speaks to you.

(1) Ask. Sister Sheri Dew shared the following in her book *Worth the Wrestle*: "In my early twenties, I admitted to a friend and mentor that I could feel the presence of the Spirit but couldn't discern specific answers. He asked me if I had asked the Lord to teach me His language—meaning, what it felt and sounded like when He was speaking to me. I hadn't, but that night I began to ask the Lord to teach me the language of revelation."[60]

Perhaps the most important thing any of us can do to increase our ability to recognize the voice of the Spirit is to ask our Heavenly Father to teach us. If you have not already, you might add this to your list of sincere questions to ask the Lord: "Can You teach me how to recognize the voice of the Holy Ghost and the answers You're trying to give me?"

(2) Counsel with others. Boyd K. Packer taught, "A testimony is to be found in the bearing of it!"[61] As we share what we know to be true, the Spirit is able to bear witness to our hearts of our own convictions and knowledge of the truth.

We don't need to bear our testimony in sacrament meeting to do this. We can counsel with others about the spiritual experiences we've had. Consider finding someone you trust—like a bishop, a friend, or a parent or other relative—whom you believe is experienced at receiving and recognizing revelation. Share the spiritual experiences you are having with them. They may be able to help you identify the presence of the Holy Ghost, and you may find that you are better able to recognize the Holy Ghost when you share your experiences with others.

(3) Practice. Beth worked very hard to give the Holy Ghost opportunities to provide her revelation. She acted on many of the principles we've discussed in this book. Reflecting on her struggle to receive

---

60. Sheri L. Dew, *Worth the Wrestle* (Salt Lake City, UT: Deseret Book, 2017), Deseret Bookshelf.

61. Boyd K. Packer, *That All May Be Edified* (Salt Lake City, UT: Bookcraft, 1982), 339–40.

a testimony of the gospel, she said, "During this time, I prayed, read the scriptures, and wrote in my journal. I also immersed myself in spiritual things like listening to talks, listening to church music, and praying often throughout the day. I was still not receiving the answer I was seeking, but I felt that my ability to feel the Spirit was increasing. I was starting to recognize the presence of the Holy Ghost."

I don't know who coined the phrase "practice makes perfect," but it has proven true in so many aspects of life. The more we practice something, the more skillful we become at it. This principle also applies to receiving and recognizing revelation. The more time we spend doing things that bring the Spirit, the more likely we are to begin to recognize the voice of the Spirit.

As you have acted in faith on the principles we've discussed, have you felt your ability to recognize the presence of the Holy Ghost increase? You may, as Beth did, pause to recognize and record how that process has taken place for you.

Waiting On the Lord

I firmly believe that the Lord will answer every sincere question we bring to Him. However, sometimes the answer we receive from heaven comes in the form of understanding and strength to move forward in faith as we wait for future information.

We all look forward to a day when our understanding will be made perfect, when all doubt and error will be removed and we shall see things as they really are. Until that time, our faith, coupled with Christ's redeeming power, can enable us to have joy in this life and prepare us for eternal life in His presence while we wait for answers. When the Lord can't yet give us the understanding and information we seek, he *can* give strength and hope.

Looking to Christ in every thought can give us the ability to patiently accept His invitation in Doctrine and Covenants 88:68: "Therefore, sanctify yourselves that your minds become single to God, and the days will come that you shall see him; for he will unveil his face unto you, and it shall be in his own time, and in his own way, and according to his own will."

Exercises

Ponder the following questions and write down your thoughts.

- What answers have you received to your sincere questions?
- What doubts have you been able to overcome and replace with faith?
- How has this experience changed your relationship with your Heavenly Father and your Savior?
- How has this experience changed you?

When Thou Art Converted

After instituting the sacrament during His final evening with His disciples, the Savior turned to Peter and said these unexpected words: "Simon, Simon, behold, Satan hath desired to have you, that he may sift you as wheat: But I have prayed for thee, that thy faith fail not: and when thou art converted, strengthen thy brethren" (Luke 22:31–32).

Peter was taken aback by these words. "Surely, I must be converted," he must have thought. Peter declared his faith and fidelity to Jesus, indicating that he was willing follow Christ both into prison and into death (see Luke 22:33). But the Savior knew that even after all Peter had seen and experienced, Peter's testimony would still be subjected to further testing. Yet the Savior's words also indicated there would come a time when Peter's doubts would be replaced with an unshakable conversion. And Christ's counsel to His beloved disciple was that when that time came, Peter was to turn his attention to helping other's obtain that same conversion and unshakable faith. We are able to see the fulfillment of Christ's words in Peter as we study his acts and words in the New Testament.

Now, we know that Peter still had much to learn and had many questions. Indeed, Peter, as leader of the Church, dealt with some of the most complex social questions of his time, not the least of which was the decision to expand the preaching of the gospel and the blessings of Church membership to the Gentile nations (see Acts 10–11). But surely Peter's exceptional experiences of learning to look to Christ in his moments of doubt, trial, and questioning were essential to developing his unshakable faith and conversion, which enabled him to bring strength to thousands of God's children.

Indeed, it would seem that the final stage in overcoming doubt, obtaining answers to the most important questions of our souls, and developing an unshakable testimony of the restored gospel is to then find joy in helping others experience the peace and joy in Christ that we now enjoy.

When Alma recounted his life-changing conversion experience to his son Helaman, he too declared the great joy he now found in helping others receive the same conversion he had obtained. He wrote:

> Yea, and from that time even until now, I have labored without ceasing, that I might bring souls unto repentance; that I might bring them to taste of the exceeding joy of which I did taste; that they might also be born of God, and be filled with the Holy Ghost.
>
> Yea, and now behold, O my son, the Lord doth give me exceedingly great joy in the fruit of my labors;
>
> For because of the word which he has imparted unto me, behold, many have been born of God, and have tasted as I have tasted, and have seen eye to eye as I have seen; therefore they do know of these things of which I have spoken, as I do know; and the knowledge which I have is of God.
>
> And I have been supported under trials and troubles of every kind, yea, and in all manner of afflictions . . . and I do put my trust in him. . . .
>
> And I know that he will raise me up at the last day, to dwell with him in glory; yea, and I will praise him forever. (Alma 26:24–28)

We began this book sharing a little of the story of my dear friend Amy, and we have referred to her experience frequently as we've discussed these principles. Amy, like so many others, truly has great faith. Amy worked hard through several months of sincere study, prayer, seeking the witness of the Holy Ghost, and keeping the commandments. She chose to exchange her doubts for sincere, seeking questions that she took to the Lord. As she did so, Amy's perceptions began to change. She began to experience and recognize God's mercy for her personally. Gradually, her doubts were replaced by revelation and life-changing personal experiences with the Holy Ghost as well as a renewed confirmation of her past experiences. Her fears and anxieties began to calm as she looked to Christ.

Perhaps the crowning moment for Amy came when she finally felt ready and prepared to return to the temple. After that beautiful experience, Amy recorded, "God is so good, and the Savior has reached down to lift and save me. I feel so humbled and so blessed and so good, and the faith and trust that I have in Him has freed my soul. I can give Him my *heart* and my *will* and my everything. This has not only affected my life but my family as well."

Such is Christ's redeeming power as we look unto Him in every thought in our lives. I have a witness that if the Lord will do that for Amy, He'll do it for you or someone you love.

Amy is open about her experience. She frequently counsels with those who are similarly passing through faith crises. Recently a Church member who was passing through their own trial of faith, and who was wondering if they would ever be able to have faith again, asked Amy, "What about now? How do your doubts affect you now?"

Amy responded, "I don't really even think about it now. It's not a thing for me anymore. I got the answers I needed."

Amy, like all of us, still has many unanswered questions. But the foundational testimony that she developed through personal experiences with heaven enables her to move forward with faith. She knows how to replace doubts with faith and sincere questions when they arise. And with that strengthened testimony and conversion, she is now able to help bring others to the Savior to experience the same joy and peace that she experienced.

As we learned at the outset of this book, doubt is something that all of us, even the most faithful of Christ's disciples, may expect to encounter. The question is not whether doubts and questions will arise but where we will look when they do. And if we, like Peter and Amy, can learn to receive the Savior's invitation to "look unto [Him] in every thought" (Doctrine and Covenants 6:36) when those moments arise, then we too can emerge with a solid, unshakable relationship with Christ that the storms and waves of doubt can no longer threaten to sink. And when that conversion occurs, we too may find the joy that comes from strengthening our brothers and sisters in that same journey.

A Personal Witness

As we now close, I feel impressed to share something about the experience of writing this book because I believe it may be personally relevant to you.

This book is full of imperfections. I've spent countless hours writing and rewriting sentences and paragraphs as I've struggled to seek the guidance of the Holy Ghost about the message I needed to deliver, and even then, I know it's imperfect. I apologize for those imperfections.

The concept for this book came from a talk I gave at a ward conference in 2015. Since that time, I have felt an unending push to try to get this message to someone who needs it. Yes, it has sadly taken years for me to write this book as I struggled to fit in an hour here and an hour there in my busy schedule—the busy life of balancing work duties, serving in church callings, and striving to fulfill my responsibilities as a husband to my faithful, beautiful wife and as a father to our four busy and amazing children.

At times, I became discouraged, thinking I would never be able to find the time to get this done. "What if nobody wants to publish it? What if nobody reads it? What if I've waited too long and the moment has passed because I didn't prioritize this?" These are all thoughts I frequently had. But every time those doubts would come and I would consider giving up on this writing, a message would come to my heart that went something like this: "If even one of My children receives this message, and is able to come unto Christ because of it, then it's all worth it. Just keep going." Now, I know that's personal revelation to me specifically, but I share it because I think there's a message in it for you.

This book is for you. I don't know who you are. I don't know who this message is meant to find. But I hope it does find you. And I want you to know that I know the Lord loves you. I have felt His love for you as I've struggled to write this book. I am again amazed at how far the Lord will go, or how far He will send one of His willing servants, to reach out to the one—one of His children who needs Him.

If anything in this book has served to remind you of who you are, to give you hope, or to bring you back to the goodness of our Savior and His restored gospel, then every moment spent in this work over the past many years has been worth it.

I give you my concluding witness that I know God lives. He knows you. He loves you. We are His children. Jesus is the Christ. He is my Redeemer and Savior and I love Him. His atoning and redeeming power are real. I know He can rescue and save each of us as we imperfectly strive to be the men and women He wants us to become. Joseph Smith was a true prophet of God, called in his weakness and imperfection to restore the gospel of Jesus Christ to the earth. The Church of Jesus Christ of Latter-day Saints is Jesus Christ's living church on the earth. The doctrine, authority, and ordinances necessary to bind us all together in love in Christ as the family of God are present on the earth today in this Church. Our Savior stands at the head of His Church and guides it today through His ordained prophet and apostles. This great work is often imperfect, challenging, and messy, but it is wonderful and oh so worth the effort.

I pray that these principles we've discussed have given you the faith and tools you need in order to move forward. I give you my witness that if you will do the work to "look unto [Christ] in every thought" (Doctrine and Covenants 6:36), He will reach back out to you with arms wide open, ready to receive you and wrap you in indescribable love. He stands ready, waiting for you to call out as Peter did, "Lord, save me" (Matthew 14:30). He can and will replace your doubts, fears, and heartaches with faith, confidence, healing, and an enduring divine witness of Jesus Christ and His restored gospel that will bring the peace you are seeking. And I give this as my witness in the name of our Lord and Savior, Jesus the Christ, Amen.

About the Author

Jakob R. Jones is a Latter-day Saint and author of several *Ensign* and *Liahona* magazine articles, including "Gathered Together in My Name" (2016), "Doubt Not, but Be Believing" (2019), and "Receive the Gift" (2020). In his service in the Church, he has served as a full-time missionary in Costa Rica, a high councilor, a bishop, and a counselor in a stake presidency.

Jakob and his wife, Stefanie, live in San Jose, CA, and are the parents of four beautiful children. By profession, Jakob is a leader in the high-tech industry of Silicon Valley where he "thrives in bringing people, processes, strategy, and technology together to find innovative solutions to complex problems."

Scan to visit

https://www.jakobrjones.com/